SOCIOLOGICAL FOUNDATIONS OF EDUCATION

SOCIOLOGICAL FOUNDATIONS OF EDUCATION

JAGDISH CHAND
Former Deputy Director of Education and
Executive Director of the Delhi Bureau of Textbooks,
Delhi Administration

ANSHAH

Anshah Publishing House

(First Published in 2010)

Rs. 695

ISBN: 978-81-8364-064-0

2014 Impression

Sociological Foundation of Education

Published by:

ANSHAH PUBLISHING HOUSE
LG 18-19, Pankaj Central Market,
Patparganj, Delhi 110092, Ph.: 22235152, 22236152
Email: info@shiprapublication.com
Website: www.shiprapublication.com

Preface

The book 'Psychological Philosophical and Sociological Foundations of Education', published in 2009 covers the emerging concerns in education presented by the changing Philosophical, Psychological and Sociological perspectives.

As per the demand in the market and requirement of curriculum in various universities, the book covering Sociological Foundations of Education is brought out independently. It is hoped that this volume will be welcomed by the readers and its advantage is also taken by the pre-service and in-service teachers.

Wide range of primary and secondary sources has been consulted and used for enriching the book, author is grateful to all the authors and their publishers.

Jagdish Chand

Contents

1

Educational Sociology

MEANING AND DEFINITION OF SOCIOLOGY

Sociology is the study of social relationships. It studies the human behaviour in groups. It relates to the social structure and social phenomenon. In its study, different forms of human interrelations are involved.

The term 'Sociology' was coined in 1838 by *August Comte* (1798-1857) of France who is considered to be the 'Father of Sociology'. It is formed by joining the Greek word 'Soclus' meaning 'Society' and the Latin word 'Logos' meaning 'Science of Study'. Thus Sociology implies a scientific discipline or science of society.

Comte was followed by an English philosopher, *Herbert Spencer* (1820-1903) who wrote his book "*Principles of Sociology*" in 1876. Spencer believed that the human individual was like the "Cell" and the society was like an "Organism" composed of different cells.

Emile Durkheim (1857-1917) of France also made valuable contribution to Sociology.

Although Sociology as a discipline is the product of the 19th century, concepts related to sociology are as old as Manu, Yajanvalkia, Kautilya, Confucious, Aristotle and Plato.

Some of the important definitions of Sociology are:

Duncan defined sociology as "the scientific study of the processes of interactions of persons."

In the words of *E. Durkheim*, "Sociology is the science of collective representation."

Gillin and Gillin state, "Sociology in its broadest sense may be said to be the study of interaction arising from the association of living beings."

Green states, "Sociology is the synthesising and generalising science of man in all his social relationships."

MacIver and Page define Sociology as "Sociology is about social relationships, the network of relationships we call society."

Max Weber, a well-known German sociologist considers Sociology to be a "science which attempts the interpretative understanding of social action."

From the above definitions of Sociology, it is clear that the central theme in Sociology is 'social interaction'. Social interaction includes interaction with cultural and other institutions, such as the family, the play and peer group, religious, economic and educational institution—in fact every form of group living. It studies the customs and traditions that grow out of these interactions, the institutions that crystallise these basic human interests and the changes that occur in these institutions. Sociology also studies the possibility of 'directing' these changes in the ultimate interest of human welfare. It helps to understand the force that 'bring changes' and also the 'effect' of these changes on behaviour and personality development in individuals. It throws light on man as a social being. It examines social changes and social control.

Sociology is subdivided into different branches of specialisation. Each branch has specialised methods of investigation and research. Important branches are:

1. Criminal Sociology.
2. Educational Sociology.
3. Industrial Sociology.
4. Medical Sociology.

5. Occupational Sociology.
6. Rural Sociology.
7. Social Stratification Sociology.
8. Urban Sociology.

MEANING OF SOCIOLOGICAL BASIS OF EDUCATION: EDUCATIONAL SOCIOLOGY

Sociological basis implies that Sociology plays an important role in determining educational issues just as philosophical, psychological, religious and scientific basis influence education, the same way sociological basis. The sociological basis of education has led to the emergence of sociology of Education or Educational Sociology. Some scholars distinguish between Educational Sociology and Sociology of Education.

E. George Payne (USA) often called the '*Father of Educational Sociology*' has given the meaning of Educational Sociology as "Educational Sociology is the science which describes and explains institutions, groups and social processes in relation to the educational system in its evolution and changing function."

Ottaway explains the meaning of Educational Sociology as "Educational Sociology starts with the assumption that education is an activity which goes on in a society, and its aims and methods depend on the nature of the society, in which it takes place."

According to *Dan W. Dodson,* "Educational Sociology is particularly interested in finding out how to manipulate the educational process to achieve better personality development."

In the words of *Brown,* "Educational Sociology is the study of interaction of the individual and his cultural environment including other individuals, social groups and patterns of behaviour."

In the words of *Good,* "Educational Sociology is the scientific study of how people live in social groups."

In the words of *Cook and Cook* "Educational Sociology is the study of human factors in the educative process, with the aim to improve teaching and learning in all types of educational systems."

Carte's view is "Educational Sociology is the study of those processes of Sociology that are significant for the educative process."

From above, it is clear that social interaction is the key problem of Educational Sociology.

Educational Sociology is the applied side of Sociology which is the study of social relationships. Social relationships are of various types and Educational Sociology covers educational relationships.

BRIEF HISTORY OF THE DEVELOPMENT OF EDUCATIONAL SOCIOLOGY

George Payne explained the various dimensions of Educational Sociology in his book '*The Principles of Educational Sociology*', published in 1928. In this book he explained the effects of learning on group life and that of the group life on learning. He further explained how education as a social process may eliminate social defects. He also described how education as a social process may strengthen desirable ideals and standards that a society aims to achieve.

John Dewey, a great American educational thinker did a lot of work to popularise the ideas of Educational Sociology through his books "Experience and Education" (1938), "Schools of Tomorrow" (1942) and "Education Today" (1949). Dewey greatly emphasised the social function of education. He considered school as a social institution which 'purifies' and 'idealises' the existing social institutions.

SCOPE OF EDUCATIONAL SOCIOLOGY

The scope of Educational Sociology is very vast. It has constantly extended its domain. Its scope now includes as stated below:

1. It includes the relation of education to various social forces, particularly culture.
2. It includes how culture is handed over to coming generations through agencies like the school, the home, the religious organisations, the play-groups etc.
3. It includes how socialisation, especially of the child takes place as a result of social interaction.
4. It includes the role of these agencies in the educational process: (a) the school, (b) the press, (c) the radio, (d) the T.V., (e) the cinema.
5. It includes education as a means of social change and social control.
6. It deals with the impact of sociological thinking on the meaning, aims and functions of education, the curriculum including co-curricular activities, social organisation and methodology of teaching.

Important Issues of Study in Educational Sociology

1. Interrelation of education and sociology.
2. Education as an instrument of social progress.
3. Place of school in society.
4. Place of a teacher in society.
5. Mutual relations of students and teachers.
6. Social life in the school.
7. School and the community.
8. School and its relations with social institutions.
9. Promotion of social feeling in the students.
10. Social aspirations, needs and problems and educational system.
11. Curriculum and the needs of the society.
12. Promotion of critical and constructive approach.
13. Social advancements.
14. Equalisation of educational opportunities.
15. Role of the mass media in education and social progress.
16. Use of group and cooperative methods of teaching.

Aims of Studying Educational Sociology

Harington has suggested the following aims of studying Educational Sociology:

1. To acquire knowledge about school work and the work of teachers in relation to society and social progress.
2. To study the impact of social elements on the school.
3. To acquire knowledge of the effects of social elements on the individual.
4. To construct curriculum with comprehensive understanding of the economic and cultural tendencies of society.
5. To gain knowledge about the democratic ideals.
6. To employ research techniques for achieving the aims of Educational Sociology.

Broad Sociological Perspective or Basis of Education

Sociological perspective of education implies the following:

1. Education is essentially a social process.
2. Education takes place only in society.
3. Social milieu (environment) itself educates the child.
4. Education has an important social role to play.
5. Education is a life-long process.
6. School is just one but the most important of all the social institutions.

IMPORTANCE OF EDUCATIONAL SOCIOLOGY: CONTRIBUTION OF EDUCATIONAL SOCIOLOGY TO EDUCATION

Educational Sociology has a great bearing on education. As a matter of fact, there is no dimension of education which has remained unaffected by Educational Sociology. It is rightly stated by Zelong, "Educational Sociology today stands at the head of a great road of high promise, the road to practical technology that may contribute vitally to the development of a new kind of education—an education that actually develops citizens who know how to take part and delight in social participation and who have developed a truly sympathetic understanding of the emotional feeling of divergent groups, from those of the social community to those of the world."

In the opinion of educational sociologists, the school is the focal point around which revolves the life of the growing child. Man is a social being. He is a member of the society. The influence of society on education is imperative. Education involves several interrelations. Education must be a social activity. Education influences the society and is also influenced by the society. Educational reforms cannot be discussed in a vacuum. Social movements make changes in educational aims, contents, methods of teaching and its organisational set up. In fact the functions of education undergo radical changes. Clarke has very rightly observed, "No writer on education can wholly shake himself free from the influence of time and place." Dewey explains how the changing society affects education in his book "The School and Society" in these words, "Whenever we have in mind the discussion of a new movement in education, it is especially necessary to take the broader social view. Otherwise, changes in the social institutions and traditions will be looked at as the arbitrary invention of particular teachers. It is only by connecting education with the general march of events that the school can lose its isolated character."

Sociology discharges five different types of functions as far as education is concerned:

1. *Technical Function*: The study of Sociology helps to determine the functions of educational institutions and also suggests why they should be improved.

2. *Introductory Function*: Sociology acquaints the people with the nature of the educational system and its processes and also indicates the directions which it should follow.

3. *Informative Function*: A scientific study of Sociology helps to get various functional information about the problems of

society and provides guidelines to education for solving problems relating to it.

4. *Cultural Function*: The study of Sociology helps to develop a cosmopolitan outlook, universal brotherhood and tolerance towards other societies and outlines the role of education in this task.

5. *Democratic Function*: The most important function discharged by Sociology is the democratic function. This democratic function of Sociology becomes the most dominant basis of education. Education is expected to provide great help in understanding the democratic structure and developing democratic skills and values in the students as well as the masses.

From above we conclude that the sociological bases of education are:

1. Education takes place in society.
2. Education is essentially a social process.
3. Social environment itself educates the child.
4. Education has a social role to play.
5. Education is a lifelong process.
6. Education is not schooling.
7. Education is formal, non-formal and informal.
8. School is not the only social institution of education. There are several other social institutions that impart education.
9. Economic and political factors of the society play a dominant role in educational reforms.
10. Education must be social in nature, i.e., it must develop democratic skills and values in the students.

Some of the important influences of Sociology are given below:

1. *Sociological Basis and the Meaning of Education*: In this regard, Brown's views have great significance. In his words,

"Education is the consciously controlled process whereby changes in behaviour are produced in the person and through the person within the group."

2. *Sociological Basis and the Aims of Education*: The development of sociological tendency in education has put special emphasis as regards aims of education.

(i) Development of social attitudes, feelings and qualities.
(ii) Development of a socially efficient individual.
(iii) Improvement in vocational efficiency.
(iv) Effective use of leisure time and development of healthy recreational pursuits.

The social aims in education finds expression in such concepts—'education for social services', 'education for citizenship', 'education for social efficiency', 'education for emotional integration', 'education for national unity', 'education for nationalism' and 'education for patriotism' etc.

Why Social Aim in Education? An individual is regarded as endowed with a social nature. He is social by nature. He resides in an intricate web of social relations. Without social relations a new born baby would almost perish. An individual cannot live and develop in isolation from society. An isolated individual is a figment of imagination. A socially efficient individual is an asset to the society. He is not a drag or parasite on any individual and society. He is able to earn his livelihood. Education, therefore, should aim at the development of the individual in such a way that he becomes a useful member of the society. He should be made aware of his rights, responsibilities and relationships while living in a group.

3. *Sociological Basis and Functions of Education*: Monroe lays down the following main functions of education.

(a) Diffusion of more and more knowledge.
(b) Education as a means of social control.
(c) Education as a means of transmission of social heritage.

(d) Education as a means of social progress.
(e) Education as a means of developing constructive and creative outlook of the individuals.

4. *Sociological Basis and the Curriculum*: The primary concern of the curriculum is the development of "We feeling—a feeling that the student belongs to the society and has a spirit of social interaction."

Brown, More and Cole point out the following principles of constructing school curriculum from the view point of sociology:

(a) Curriculum should be based on the conditions, problems and needs of society.
(b) It should be based on the real concerns and problems of pupils.
(c) It should reflect the basic cultural values of the society it serves.
(d) It should be an agent in the transmission of the highest values of the culture.
(e) It should provide educational programmes and activities that give them wholesome participating roles in society. This participation is conducive to the development of responsible citizenship.
(f) The curriculum must be functional in its relation to adult living and concurrently be adapted to the level of development of the child.
(g) The school programme should treat with dignity all worthwhile vocations and services in community life.
(h) The curriculum should develop healthy attitudes regarding human relations.
(i) It should prepare the child for the world society.
(j) It should prepare socially efficient individuals.
(k) It should be flexible and changeable for the effective realisation of socially determined objectives.
(l) It should lead to the development of genuine 'We

feeling'—"a feeling that the student belongs to the group and has a spirit of social interaction."

5. *Sociological Basis and Methods of Teaching*: The following are the sociological basis of the methods of teaching:

(a) The methods of teaching should enable the pupil to acquire those skills and knowledge in the classroom which are helpful to him in his adjustment to social situations.
(b) The methods of teaching must seek to utilise the social forces operating in the social life with a view of developing a capacity for social adjustment.
(c) The methods should develop problem-solving and constructive thinking.
(d) The socialised techniques, the project and group methods, by and large should replace the lecture and recitation method.

6. *Sociological Basis and the Role of the Teacher*: It is said that the destiny of a nation is shaped in its classroom and it is the teacher who is a very important instrument in moulding that destiny. To be able to discharge such a high responsibility, it is very necessary that the teacher must become conscious of his role towards society. His behaviour should indicate his attempt to do his job properly. His personality must reflect characteristics of good citizenship. The teacher himself must be exposed to the concept of freedom, egalitarianism, dignity of the individual, rights and duties etc. so that he may transmit the same to the younger generation.

The educational sociologists consider teacher as a 'social engineer'—an engineer who can play an important role in social reconstruction. The Educational Commission (1964-66) observed that the "destiny of India is being shaped in its classroom." It is therefore, the teacher who is an important instrument in shaping the destiny through his influence on the children. A teacher is expected to:

(a) Possess right attitude of social behaviour.
(b) Remain above casteism, regionalism, etc.
(c) Give due regard to the dignity of the pupils.

7. *Sociological Basis and the School*: Dewey's ideal school is expected to perform the following functions:

(a) Reflecting and epitomising the larger society outside its walls.
(b) Purifying the activities of the society in its environment.
(c) Simplifying the activities of the society in its environment.
(d) Balancing the activities of the society in its environment.

8. *Sociological Basis and the Discipline*: Discipline is social through and through. It should come through participation in group activities and social service activities.

Summing up. Sociology shapes education and forms a vital force in the entire framework of education. The whole superstructure of education has depended upon social forces, needs and demands. The expectations and aspiration of a changing society are reflected through the educational system of a country or a nation. Thus, we can hardly afford to think of education in isolation today. Clarke has rightly stated, "No writer on education, however much he strive for after universal thought can wholly shake himself free from the influence of time and place."

Society is dynamic, it grows and changes and as such these social changes must not only be reflected in education but also must affect it. It is only by connecting education with the general march of events that the school can lose its isolated character. As Dewey has stated, "School must become the child's habitat to be a miniature community, an embryonic society."

2

Education as an Instrument of Social Change: Role of the School

In simple words, social change implies change in the social structure and functions of the various units which form society. Social structure includes social institutions like the family, the marriage system, caste system, educational institutions, customs, manners, literacy forms, language, dress and food habits etc.

The following definitions of social change explain the various dimensions of social change:

1. *Prof. R.B. Mathur* explained the concept of social change in "*The Third India Year book of Education—Educational Research* (1964)" in these words, "Social change refers to the modifications in the organisation and behaviour of the group as expressed in its laws, institutions, customs, modes and beliefs. The change may be gradual or sudden, evolutionary or revolutionary. When change is supposedly for the better, it becomes 'progress' which is essentially an evolutionary concept."

2. According to *B. Kuppaswami*, "When we speak of social change we might assert that there is some change in social behaviour and in the social structure."

3. *Herry Johnson* would like to include five kinds of changes under social change: (a) change in social values; (b) institutional changes; (c) change in distribution of possessions and rewards; (d) change in personnel; and (e) change in abilities or attitudes of personnel.

4. *Kingslay Davis* defines social change as, "Only such alterations as occur in social organisation, i.e., in the structure and functions of society."

5. *Prof. S.P. Ruhela* views social change as "The term social change might imply changes in social attitudes, behaviour, customs, habits, manners, relations and values of people, in social institutions and structures, in the ways or styles of living."

6. According to *MacIver and Page*, "Social change is a process responsive to many types of changes, to changes in the man-made condition of living, to changes in the attitude of man and changes that go beyond human control to the biological and physical nature."

7. *Delbert C. Miller* observes, "Social change refers to a pattern of social relationship in a given social setting, which exhibits changes over some definite period of time."

8. *Sir Jones* states, "Social change is a term used to describe variation in or modification of any aspect of social processes, social interactions or social organisation."

9. *Fairchild* has stated, "Social change means variations or modifications in any aspect of social process, patterns or forms."

10. *Dawson and Getlys* observe, "Cultural change is social change since culture is social in its origin."

11. *Merril and Eldredge* have defined social change as, "Social change means that large number of persons are engaged in activities that differ from those which they or their immediate forefathers engaged in sometime before. When human behaviour is in the process of modification, that is only another way of indicating that social change is occurring."

12. *Gillen and Gillen* observe, "Social changes are variations from the accepted modes of life whether due to alterations in geographical conditions, in cultural equipment, composition of the population or ideologies and whether brought about by diffusion or intervention within the group."

SIGNIFICANT FEATURES OF SOCIAL CHANGE AND ELEMENTS

1. Social change may mean discarding some old elements or old things.
2. Social change may mean addition of new elements or things.
3. Social change may be sudden or slow.
4. All aspects or elements may not change at the same rate.
5. Social change may be brought about by violent or non-violent means.
6. Social change may be planned or unplanned.
7. Social change is fairly lasting.
8. Social change sets a trend.
9. Social change is revealed in the social relations and values.
10. Social change affects a sizeable population of the society.
11. Social change may be caused by internal factors, i.e., factors inside the society and external factors, i.e., factors outside the society.
12. Social change may be complex.

Main Elements of Social Change

(1) *Changes in Social Structures*

This includes changes in

(i) Class structure

(ii) Caste systems

(iii) System of land tenure, e.g., changes in the Zamindar system

(iv) Labour conditions

(vi) Institutional structure in the school

(2) *Changes in Social Behaviour*

(i) Customs

(ii) Food habits

(iii) Intermingling

(iv) Speech habits

(v) Openness and broadmindedness

Patterns of Social Change

MacIver and Page list three patterns of social change as shown below:

Patterns of Social Change

(1) *Cumulative Change*
Later social changes based on earlier social changes

(2) *Social Change in Reverse Direction*
Change in upward direction but afterwards reversal of direction

(3) *Wave-like Social Change*
Alternating ups and down in social change

Some Examples of Factors Affecting Social Change

1. Disappearance of the Indus Valley Civilisation/Society probably on account of natural factors like floods.
2. Changes in Indian Society as a result of religious and social movements, influence of Buddhism etc.
3. Social changes in India on account of political domination of the British over India and India's independence.
4. Social changes in India on account of the impact of ICT.

PROCESS OF SOCIAL CHANGE

Process of social change may be classified in a number of ways:

Process of Social Change: Classification I

- Planned Process of Social Change
- Unplanned Process of Social Changes

Process of Social Change: Classification II

- Non-violent Process of Social Change
- Violent Process of Social Change

Process of Social Change: Classification III

- Evolutionary Process of Social Change
- Revolutionary Process of Social Change

Process of Social Change: Classification IV

- Man-made Process of Social Change
- Natural or Geographical Process of Social Change (The Indus Valley Civilization Vanished Perhaps on Account of Floods or some Natural Calamity)

CAUSES/FACTORS OF SOCIAL CHANGE

There are a large number of causes or factors that bring about social change. Sometimes even one cause may become responsible for social change. At other times, some factors or causes jointly act in such a way that social change becomes inevitable. Again it is stressed that the processes, causes and effects of social change work simultaneously.

Ideas and ideologies of great leaders have played an important role in social change. The influence of prominent personalities like Marx and Lenin in Russia, Mao Tse Tung in China and Gandhiji in India are some of the well-known examples of modern history which led to social changes.

Ideas like 'Liberty', 'Equality' and 'Fraternity' were great forces in giving birth to French Revolution which in turn immensely changed the French society.

The Important Factors of Social Change with Special Reference to India

1. Demographic
2. Geographical/National
3. Globalisation
4. Hinduisation
5. Indianisation
6. Information and Communication Technology

7. Industrialisation
8. Liberalisation
9. Modernisation
10. Nationalisation
11. Politicalisation
12. Privatisation
13. Sanskritisation
14. Secularisation
15. Social mobility or socialisation
16. Spiritualisation
17. Urbanisation
18. Westernisation

Note: Some factors may be more prominent in playing their role in social change. Some may come into conflict. Some may play their role in an invisible manner. Parson has very rightly observed, "There is the plurality of possible origin of social change."

A brief analysis of some factors of social change is given here:

1. *Demographic Factors*: Increase or decrease in population has an immediate effect upon social change. Partition of India leading to unprecedented migration led to several changes in Indian society.
2. *Geographical Factors*: It is said that on account of floods or some other natural phenomenon, Indus Valley Civilisation came to an end.
3. *Hinduisation*: This process of social change consists of the attempts of many tribal communities in India to enter the broad field of Hindu social structure. Also attempts are made to popularise Hindu beliefs and customs etc.
4. *Indianisation*: This is the process of social change in which several people belonging to different faiths, tend to identify themselves with Indian culture. In several catholic churches in South India and elsewhere, it is observed that many nuns wear Indian dresses—sarees and blouses. Worship is also done in Indian style. Lamps, candles, incense, 'prasad' etc. are used in the Indian style. Instead of English, regional languages are used in religious songs and prayers.
5. *Industrialisation*: Industrialisation has also given rise to social changes like, drinking, trade union activities, growth of slums, educational institutions, banks, roads etc.

6. *Modernisation*: Modernisation is a process of social change which emphasises rational, secular and scientific approach.
7. *Politicisation*: It is the process of social change through the spread of knowledge about political ideologies, parties and leaders. In this process of social change, people become aware of their rights and responsibilities.
8. *Sanskritisation*: In this process, low caste Hindu or tribe or other group attempts to change its customs, ideologies, rituals and ways of life in the direction of a high caste.
9. *Secularisation*: Movements like Arya Samaj and Brahmo Samaj have promoted the process of secularisation. It is a process of change which views events, things and ideals from a rational point of view.
10. *Social Mobility*: Social mobility is the process of change in status.
11. *Urbanisation*: This is the process of social change which has led to continuous migration from rural areas to towns. This results in the same social problems as industrialisation.
12. *Westernisation*: This is the process of social change in India which has influenced culture, living styles, values etc. of the Indian people as a result of western impact, especially during the British rule.

13 to 17. *Globalisation, Nationalisation, Privatisation and Spiritualisation*: The influence of these factors is discussed separately.

BARRIERS TO SOCIAL CHANGE

(1)	(2)	(3)	(4)	(5)	(6)	(7)	(8)
Conservative Nature of Society	Cultural Barriers	Economic Barriers	Illiteracy	Lack of Means of Communication	Political Barriers	Psychological Barriers	Religious Barriers

EDUCATION AND SOCIAL CHANGE

INTER-RELATIONSHIP BETWEEN EDUCATION AND SOCIAL CHANGE

Education is an Agent of Social Change

At the same time it is influenced by social change. This relationship functions in three ways.

1. Education as a condition of social change.
2. Education as an instrument of social change.
3. Education as a result of social change.

Education is Both Retrospective and Prospective

Education is both a creation and creator of social change. It is both conservative and progressive. Education transmits the culture of one generation to another. The rising generation has not only to be conveyed the activities and experiences of the past generation and asked to carry on those activities but it has also to be asked to make necessary changes in these activities and experiences to meet the new situations which it will meet. An integration of the old must take place with the new ones. It must be remembered that the communities live in the present, on the past and for the future. This means that activities and experiences in the present have to be built on the past and the present will guide the activities of the future. Thus, education is continuous, reorganisation and integration of activities and experiences. Education is a constructive agency for improving our society. Brown has stated, "Education brings changes in behaviour, and if its main functions are to remain mere transmission or enrichment of culture, it will fall short of its role in a dynamic society. Education must also provide situations at all age levels but within the maturity and ability of the individual to stimulate a creativeness of mind, which can explore new horizons and bring the vision of the future into a living reality."

Impact of Social Change on Education

Social change exercises a great influence on all the dimensions of education—aims, curriculum, methods of teaching, discipline etc. For instance under the British rule, the society was geared to meet the requirements of the colonial powers and accordingly education system became subservient to social changes. Likewise, after independence, an altogether a new social system emerged. This led to far-reaching changes in the educational system.

EDUCATIONAL IMPLICATIONS FOR BRINGING ABOUT SOCIAL CHANGE IN A DEMOCRATIC SET UP

1. Promotion of Democratic Values.
2. Development of Human Resources.
3. Development of Physical Resources.
4. Ensuring Equality of Opportunity.
5. Ensuring Dignity of Labour.
6. Developing Values of National Unity and Emotional Integration.
7. Fostering Scientific Values.
9. Promoting Secular Values.
9. Balancing Material, Scientific and Spiritual Values.
10. Developing World Outlook.
11. Providing Education for All, i.e., Universal Elementary Education and Adult Education.

EDUCATION AS AN INSTRUMENT OF SOCIAL CHANGE

Gandhiji wanted to bring about a silent social revolution in India through the basic system of education. In his words, "The Basic school should be the spearhead of a non-violent social revolution."

The role of education in the process of social change has been envisaged by J.S. Brubacher in these words, "If the lamp of reason is not lit or if the light is blown out, but it remains to struggle. When rational processes are put aside, it is only too likely that clubs and machine guns will become the social arbiters. Bullets will replace ballots. What a confession of intellectual and moral bankruptcy? And at what a cost?"

According to *H.C. Dent*, "A national system of education has two vital functions to perform—a traditional preservation function and a growth facilitating function. In a time of social flux both these functions become overwhelmingly important."

It is not without reason that the report of the Education Commission 1964-66 begins with these words, "The destiny of India is now being shaped in her classrooms. This, we believe, is no mere rhetoric." Education Commission has further observed that realisation of country's aspiration involves changes in the knowledge, skills, interests and values of the people as a whole. This is basic to every programme of social and economic betterment of which India stands in need. It has pointed out this fact as "If this change on a grand scale is to be achieved without violent revolution (and even then it would still be necessary) there is one instrument, and one instrument only that can be used, Education. Other agencies may help, and can indeed sometimes have a more apparent impact. But the national system of education is the only instrument that can reach all the people. It is a difficult instrument whose effective use requires strength of will, 'dedicated' work and sacrifice. But it is a sure and tried instrument, which has served other countries well in their struggle for development. It can, given the will and the skill, do so for India."

The International Commission on the Development of Education (1972) expressed its views, "Education must recognise itself for what it is: it may be the product of history and society, but it is not their passive play thing. It is an essential factor in shaping the future, particularly at the present moment, since in the last resort education has to prepare mankind to adapt the change, the predominant characteristic of our time... It has to prepare for change, show people how to accept them and benefit for them, create a dynamic, non-conformist, non-conservative frame of mind. Concurrently, it has to play the part of an antidote to the many discussions within man and society."

Education is the fulcrum upon which hangs the peaceful and evolutionary transition of society. It can ensure that the gap between reality and ideas does not become so great that it can be bridged only by revolutions which make a clean break with the past. Hence, education is not to be thought of merely as the passing on of the cumulative wisdom of society to the next generation. This will necessarily imply far-reaching changes in education and educational techniques.

The National Policy of Education in India (1986 and amended in 1992), in its introductory remarks highlighted the role of education in these words, "Education has continued to evolve, diversify and extend its reach and coverage since the dawn of human history. Every country develops its system of education to express and promote its unique socio-cultural identity and also to meet the challenges of the times. There are moments in history when a new direction has to be given to an age-old process. That moment is today."

Two-fold Functions of Education in Social Change

The problem of education in relation to social change is two-fold:

1. Adjustment to the changing situation.
2. Creation of a new order through change in knowledge, new ideas and or in other words education for social progress.

AGENCIES OF EDUCATION AND SOCIAL CHANGE

In the words of Dewey, "By various agencies, unintentional and designed, a society transforms of its own resources and ideals. Education is thus a fostering, a venturing and a cultivated process. All these words mean that it implies attention to the conditions of growth. When we have the outcome of the process in mind we speak of education as shaping, forming, moulding activity—that is a shaping into the standard form of social activity."

Types of Agencies of Education Contributing to School Change

(1) *Formal Agencies of Education*	(2) *Informal Agencies of Education*	(3) *Non-formal Agencies of Education*
1. Schools	1. Home	1. Correspondence Course
2. Colleges	2. Peer Group	2. Adult Education Centres
3. Institutions of Higher Education	3. Library	3. Open Schools
	4. Reading Room	4. Open University
	5. Social Clubs	5. Distance Education
	6. Press	6. Continuing Classes
	7. Films	7. Church
	8. Radio	
	9. T.V.	
	10. Internet etc.	
	11. Play Groups	
	12. Youth Organizations	
	13. Telephone (Mass Media includes telegraphy, telephone, radio, movies, T.V. etc.)	

SCHOOL AS A SOCIAL INSTITUTION AND AN AGENT OF SOCIAL CHANGE AND THE ROLE OF THE TEACHER

Mere conservation of the culture is not enough. Ryburn feels, "The progressive school can never be content that the present generation should simply remain where their forefathers were."

Dewey observes, "The school is primarily a social institution."

The future of mankind depends upon the education imparted in schools, "A world whose schools are unreformed is an unreformed world," writes *H.G. Wells*. This shows to what extent proper organisation of a school is necessary.

According to *K.G. Saiyidain*, the school is a centre of vigorous life. It is in direct intimate contact with the realities of the life around, reflecting the best and worthiest of its features which are simple enough to appeal to the child.

The Secondary Education Commission (1952-53) outlines the functions of the school as, "The secondary school must make itself responsible for equipping its students adequately with civic as well as vocational efficiency—and the qualities of character that go with it—so that they may be able to play their part worthily and competently in the improvement of national life. They should no longer emerge as helpless, shiftless individuals who do not know what to do themselves."

The Education Commission (1964-66) observed, "The destiny of India is now being shaped in her classroom." This clearly explains the significant role of the school in social change.

P.C. Nunn describes the role of the school in these words, "A nation's school... are an organ of its life, whose special function is to consolidate its spiritual strength, to maintain its historical continuity, to secure its past achievements, to guarantee its future. Through its schools a nation should become conscious of the abiding sources from which the best movements in its life have always taken their aspiration, should come to share the dreams of its nobler sons, should constantly submit itself to self-criticism, should purge its ideals, should reinform and redirect impulses."

S. Balakrishna Joshi sums up the concept of a school as, "A well-conducted school is a happy home, a sacred shrine, a social centre, and a society in miniature and a bewitching *Brindavan*, all beautifully blended into a synthetic structure."

P.C. Wren describes the functions of a school as "Organise the school to benefit the scholar, to train his faculties, to widen his outlook, cultivate his mind, to form and strengthen his character, to develop and cultivate his aesthetic sense, to build up his body, give his health and strength, to teach him his duty to himself, to the community and the state, in short to make an honest, capable and healthy man of him—organise the school for this and not to prepare him for the matriculation examination."

Elements in the School Contributing to Social Change

(1) School Climate and Environment
(2) Contents of the Curriculum
(3) Methodology of Instruction
(4) School Discipline
(5) Co-curriculum Programme
(6) Teacher's Attitude
(7) Self-Government in School
(8) Schools Relation with the Community
(9) Provision of Rich and Varied Facilities

The school is a social institution set up by the society to train and discipline its future citizens in certain forms of activities. It must play a major role in moulding the ideas, habits and attitudes of children with a view to producing well-balanced personalities, physically strong, mentally alert, emotionally stable, culturally sound and socially efficient.

Programmes of the School in Social Change

1. *Providing Balanced, Purified and Simplified Environment*: According to Prof. Dewey, the function of the school is to simplify, purify and balance the activities of the society. The school curriculum should reflect all this.

2. *Training in Art of Living Together*: The school activities should provide training in the art of living together.

3. *Making Provision for Experimentation*: The school laboratory will not be a toy-affair, where a few simple and carefully planned experiments are performed under vigilant eye of the teacher who sees that the prescribed routine is followed. It will endeavour to give them something of the thrill and joy of discovery and the educative experience of learning through trial and error.

4. *Developing Opportunities for Self-Discipline*: Discipline in the school will not be a matter of arbitrary rules and regulations enforced through the authority of the teachers helped by the lure of reward or the fear of punishment. The students will be given full freedom to organise functions, to conduct many of the school activities through their own committees and even to deal with certain types of disciplinary cases. In this way, discipline will be maintained through the influence of the social group and it will gradually lead to the development of self-discipline.

5. *Developing Child's Entire Personality*: School should provide a richly varied pattern of activities to cater to the development of its children's entire personality. It has to formulate a scheme of hobbies, occupations and projects that will appeal to draw out hidden powers of children of varying temperaments and aptitudes.

6. *Providing a Stimulating Environment*: The primary concern of the school should be to provide for its pupils a rich, pleasant and stimulating environment which will evoke their manifold interests and make life a matter of joyful experience.

7. *Transforming itself into an Activity School*: The school must be transformed into an "activity school" because activity has an irresistible appeal for every normal child and is his natural path to the goal of knowledge and culture.

8. *Training in Democratic Living*: We have embarked upon a new way of life, i.e., democratic way of life. So for bringing about social change (commensurate with this) schools should incorporate such activities as 'student self-government'.

9. *Developing Scientific Outlook*: Emphasis on all school programmes should be laid in the development of scientific temper in the minds of the students.

10. *School as a Centre of Community Service*: School must provide opportunities to the community to use its resources.

11. *School and Social Service*: From time to time, the students should be provided opportunities to undertake social service activities.

TEACHER AS A SOCIAL ENGINEER AND AN AGENT OF SOCIAL CHANGE

1. *Prof. Ottaway* thinks that teachers in the school can have a very powerful influence in the community they choose. Teachers' professional organisations and unions are among the orthodox pressure groups and they can bring their views before public opinion and government.

2. *The McNair Report on the Training of Teachers in England* states, "It is a truism to say that every teacher, in however humble a capacity he or she may be serving, is directly and vocationally involved in moulding the shape of things to come." "If that truism be true", observes Prof. W.O. Lester Smith of the London University; "the unsettled times in which our young citizens are going to live their lives make it necessary that those who aspire to teach should have thought and should continue to think about the problems of society with all the intelligence at their work."

3. An American educationist, *Edmund W. Gordon* has pointed out, "It is the task of the teacher to educate—to educate for change—to educate through change—to educate for orderly planned revolution. If necessary, to educate through more disruptive revolutionary action."

4. In the words of *H.G. Wells* (1886-1946), the noted historian and thinker "The teacher is the real maker of history."

5. According to *Dr. S. Radhakrishnan*, "He acts as the pivot for the transmission of intellectual erudite and technical skills from generation to generation, and helps to keep the lamp of civilisation burning. He not only guides the individuals, but also to say shapes the destiny of the nation."

6. *The National Commission on School Teachers* (1983-85) states, "We underscore that the prime task of the teacher is concerned with man-making namely the making of the India of tomorrow."

7. *The National Commission on Teachers for Higher Education* (1983-85) writes, "Teacher is an agent of change."

Ways of Playing the Role of Social Engineer by the Teacher

A teacher can convey and disseminate attitudes and values to the students through the following ways:

(i) Direct teaching.
(ii) Providing opportunities to the students for living and practising the virtues of secularism, socialism and democracy.
(iii) Teacher himself becoming models embodying the desired attitudes and values.
(iv) Undertaking social awakening programmes.

Desired Competency in the Teacher to Play the Role in Social Change

It is said that the destiny of a nation is shaped in its classroom and it is the teacher who is a very important instrument in moulding that destiny. To be able to discharge such a big responsibility, it is very necessary that the teacher must become conscious of his role towards society. His behaviour must indicate his attempt to do his job properly. His personality must reflect characteristics of good citizenship. The teacher himself must be exposed to the concepts of freedom, equalitarianism, dignity of the individual, rights and duties etc. so that he may transmit the same to the younger generation.

Constraints on the Teachers to Play Their Role in Social Change

Prof. S.P. Ruhela and K.C. Vyas pose this question in the context of Indian situation, "How can they be so when the occupation of school teachers has so far not been able to emerge as a profession in the strict sense of the term due to their effective unenlightened and uncommitted professional organisations, and when many teachers' training institutions still continue to be disgusting educational slums, concentration camps, factionalism and inaction, in which teachers are very poorly socialised, trained and motivated to think and act creatively or innovate."

LIMITATIONS OF EDUCATION IN BRINGING ABOUT CHANGES

1. *Limited Resources*: Adequate funds are needed for providing educational facilities on a large scale. Besides funds are needed for qualitative improvement of education. Ill-equipped individuals cannot bring about social changes in the society.

2. *Attitude of 'No Change'*: People in general and even educated people are reluctant to follow new paths.

3. *Poverty and Ignorance of the Masses*: Percentage of literacy remained very low in India for a number of years. It is only recently that considerable improvement has become visible. Likewise a substantial percentage of people are still below the poverty line. In such a situation, social reforms take place very slowly.

4. *Lack of 'Political Will'*: Revolutionary constructive educational reforms could not be carried out on account of the non-availability of necessary political support. Thus education remained ineffective to a considerable extent in playing its role in social change.

Summing Up: We may sum up the role of education and the school with the views of two great thinkers. *M.V. Jeffreys* has observed, "It is hard to realise, in our own day, the magnitude of the revolution of which the schools were the instrument. It is not only that the mass of people have been taught to read and write and that the universities are open to talent. What has happened in a social revolution, in which cultural authority has shifted from family and social tradition to school... the agency of social revolution was education."

There are educationists and thinkers like Philip Coombs who think otherwise. They think that the notion that education can change the society is an illusion. To quote *Philip Coombs*, "Education is not a cure for all the ills of the world anymore than it is responsible for causing them. Education at best has at its disposal only limited time and means for satisfying all the expectations that individuals and society bring to the educational process."

SOCIAL CHANGE AND EDUCATION OF THE MASSES

Stressing the importance of the poor, *Swami Vivekananda* said, "If the poor boy cannot come to the education, education must go to him." Swami Vivekananda realised the importance of the education of neglected sections of the society and their contribution to national welfare. He wrote, "There are thousands of single minded, self-sacrificing sanyasins in our own country, going from village to village, teaching religion. If some of them can be organised as teachers of secular things also, they will go from place to place, from door to door, not only preaching but teaching also. Suppose two of these may go to a village in the evening with a camera, a globe, some maps, etc. They can teach a great deal of astronomy and geography to the ignorant. By telling stories about different nations, they can give the poor a hundred times more information throughout the year than they can get in life time through books. Kindle their knowledge with the help of modern science. Teach them history, geography, science, literature and along with these the profound truths of religion through these." All this implies in the present situation, a programme of functional social education. Such a programme is likely to develop new approach to understand the issues of national development. It is also likely to develop their capacity to produce more. They will learn the use of new implements—agricultural and industrial. They will have a better standard of life and living. Thus they will contribute to national welfare.

EDUCATION OF THE DEPRIVED SECTIONS OF THE SOCIETY

A society is composed of several sections. There are some sections of the society which come under the category of deprived sections. Without their welfare, national welfare cannot be imagined. Education is considered as an important instrument of their welfare.

The National Policy on Education has observed, "In our national perception, education is essentially for all. This is fundamental to our all-round development, material and spiritual." PART IV of the National Policy on Education, titled 'Education for Equality', includes several programmes for removing disparities and to equate educational opportunities by attending to the specific needs of those who have been denied equality so far. It lists special measures for the speedy promotion of education of the following categories:

1. Education for Women's Equality.
2. The Education of Scheduled Castes.
3. The Education of the Scheduled Tribes.
4. Other Educationally Backward Sections and Areas.
5. The Minorities.
6. The Handicapped.

3

Education and National Development

MEANING OF NATIONAL DEVELOPMENT

The term national development is very comprehensive. It includes all aspects of the life of an individual and the nation—cultural, democratic, economic, educational, emotional, material, moral, physical, spiritual and social. All aspects of development are very important and interrelated also. If one aspect remains undeveloped, others are also affected. National development is not synonymous with economic development though economic development is an important facet of national development.

The United Nation Decade Report has defined it as, "National Development is growth plus change. Change in turn is social and cultural as well as economic and qualitative as well as quantitative."

It is truism to say that is hardly a dimension of national life which is not influenced by education in one form or the other.

Problems of National Development in India

Although India has made a tremendous progress in all areas of national life since independence, still much remains to be done. Industrialised and several developed countries are far ahead of India in national development. Nearly 26 per cent population is below the poverty line. About one-third population is literate. Life expectancy is also quite lower. Infant mortality under one year is high. Net primary enrolment attendance is below average. It is, therefore, important that deficiencies in the planning process need to overcome as speedily as possible. Increase in growth rate of economy has little significance when a substantial percentage of population does not get the benefit of development of economy. On the whole it can be said that strenuous efforts are needed to achieve the desired objectives of national development.

CHIEF CHARACTERISTICS OF A DEVELOPING AND A DEVELOPED SOCIETY

The chief characteristics of a developed and a developing society are broadly as under:

Developed Society	*Developing Society*
1. Very high gross national net product (GNP) per capita.	1. Low GNP per capita.
2. Very low infant mortality rate (number of deaths of infants).	2. High infant mortality rate.
3. High adult literacy.	3. Low adult literacy.
4. High life expectancy.	4. Low life expectancy.
5. High percentage of schooling (completing primary and secondary state).	5. Low percentage of schooling.
6. Very low drop-out rates.	6. High drop-out rates.
7. Industry dominated economy.	7. Agriculture dominated economy.
8. High percentage of urban population.	8. High percentage of rural population.
9. Population growth rate is low.	9. Population growth rate is high.
10. Most of the population can afford items of comfort.	10. Most of the people cannot afford such items.

(*Contd.*)

Developed Society	*Developing Society*
11. Distribution of income is fairly even.	11. Most people are poor.
12. People are engaged in gainful employment.	12. Relatively there is more unemployment and under employment.
13. Production in the farms and factories is done by the latest modern techniques.	13. The techniques of agricultural and production are primitive in general.
14. People in general are not superstitious.	14. People in general are ignorant and superstitious.

INDIA'S NATIONAL DEVELOPMENT VIS-À-VIS WORLD (AROUND 2007)

Indicator	*India*	*Developing Countries*	*World*	*Industrialised Countries*
1. Under 5 (years) Mortality Rate	76	83	72	09
2. Infant Mortality Rate Under 1 Year	43	57	52	05
3. GNI Per Capita (US$)	820	1900	750	37,000
4. Life Expectancy at Birth (Years)	64	66	68	79
5. Total Adult Literacy Rate %	61%	76%	78%	99
6. Net Primary Enrolment Attendance	76	84	82	96
7. Percentage of Population Below $1 a Day 1995-2005	34	19	20	NA

Source: The State of the World's Children 2008.

Observations on National Development

Although India has made a tremendous progress in all areas of national life, still much remains to be done.

PROBLEMS OF NATIONAL DEVELOPMENT

1. Low production.
2. Low per capita income.
3. Low standards of life of the people.
4. Conservative society.
5. Danger to emotional and national integration.
6. Slow progress in universalisation of elementary education.
7. Low adult literacy rate.
8. Low standard of education
9. Population explosion
10. Decline in democratic, secular and social values.
11. Bringing about a synthesis between moral and scientific values.
12. Lack of equality of opportunity.
13. Wide gap between the rich and the poor.

SIGNIFICANT ROLE OF EDUCATION IN NATIONAL DEVELOPMENT

It is not without significance that the report of the Education Commission 1964-66 has been titled as *Education and National Development*. The Education Commission has observed, "If the pace of national development is to be accelerated, there is need for a well-defined, bold and imaginative educational policy and for determined and vigorous action to vitalise, improve and expand education."

The Commission further observed that education cannot be considered in isolation or planned in a vacuum. It has to be used as a powerful instrument of social, economic and political change and will, therefore, have to be related to the long-term national aspirations and the programmes of national development on which the country is engaged and the difficult short-term problems it is called upon to face.

The Commission has rightly observed, "In a world based

on science and technology it is education that determines the level of prosperity, welfare and security of the people. On the quality and number of persons coming out of our schools and colleges will depend our success in the great enterprise of national reconstruction whose principal objective is to raise the standard of living of our people."

The National Policy on Education (NPE) 1986 has observed, "The country has reached a stage in its economic and technical development when a major effort must be made to derive the maximum benefit from the assets already created and to ensure that the fruits of change reach all sections. Education is the highway to that goal." The modified NPE 1992 also endorsed the above statement.

Regarding the special role of higher education in national development, NPE has observed, "Higher education provides people with an opportunity to reflect on the critical social, cultural, moral and spiritual issues facing humanity. It contributes to national development through dissemination of specialised knowledge and skills."

ROLE OF EDUCATION IN SOLVING PROBLEMS OF NATIONAL DEVELOPMENT

1. To develop such skills which lead to increased production.
2. To modernise Indian society.
3. To promote values of emotional and social integration.
4. To promote democratic ideals.
5. To promote socialism.
6. To strengthen secular values.
7. To inculcate ideas of international understanding.
8. To promote the small family norm.
9. To develop environmental awareness.
10. To bring about a synthesis between cultural values and scientific values.
11. To prepare individuals for self-employment.

12. To prepare manpower needed for different areas of national life.
13. To develop spirit of service.
14. To develop sensitivity towards performing one's duties as stated in the Constitution.
15. To provide equality of opportunity for the optimum development of one's personality.

It may be emphasised that problems of national development are interrelated and areas overlap.

ROLE OF EDUCATION IN INCREASING PRODUCTION

Following recommendations are made for making education to fulfil this task:

(i) Making science as a basic component to education and culture.
(ii) Introducing socially useful productive work as an integral part of general education.
(iii) Vocationalising education, especially at the Senior Secondary School level to meet the needs of industry, agriculture and trade.
(iv) Improving scientific and technological education and research at the university stage with special emphasis on agriculture and allied science.

ROLE OF EDUCATION IN THE MODERNISATION OF INDIAN SOCIETY

Education should perform the following:

(i) Adopting new methods of teaching.
(ii) Awakening of curiosity, the development of proper interest, attitudes and values and the building up of such essential skills as independent study and capacity to think and judge for oneself.

(iii) Changing the composition of the intelligentsia; educating people of all strata of society.
(iv) Emphasising vocational subjects, science education and research.
(v) Establishing major universities of the excellence in the country.

ROLE OF EDUCATION IN PROMOTING SOCIAL AND NATIONAL INTEGRATION

The following steps are recommended:

(i) Introducing a common school system of public education.
(ii) Making social and national service an integral part of education at all stages.
(iii) Developing all modern Indian languages.
(iv) Taking necessary steps to enrich Hindi as quickly as possible so that it is able to function effectively as the official language of the Union.
(v) Encouraging and enabling students to participate in community living on the school or college campus.

ROLE OF EDUCATION IN DEVELOPING DEMOCRATIC VALUES

Education should aim at the development of democratic values through the following:

1. Organising student self-government in schools.
2. Decentralising educational management.

ROLE OF EDUCATION IN ESTABLISHING A SOCIALISTIC PATTERN OF SOCIETY

The educational system should provide for:

(i) Equality of opportunity in education.
(ii) Common school system.

(iii) Compulsory social and national service.
(iv) Liberal provision of scholarships.

ROLE OF EDUCATION IN DEVELOPING SECULAR OUTLOOK

Following steps are needed:

(i) Introducing instruction in moral, social and spiritual values.
(ii) Providing syllabus giving well-chosen information about each of the major religions of the world.
(iii) Encouraging students to meet in groups for silent meditation.
(iv) Presenting before students high ideals of social justice and social service.

ROLE OF EDUCATION IN PROMOTING INTERNATIONAL UNDERSTANDING

This could be done by taking the following steps:

(i) Revising of textbooks and elimination of hostile material about other communities.
(ii) Organising inter-country student exchange programme.
(iii) Celebrating UN days.

4

Social Justice and Equality: Role of Education

(Empowerment of SCs, STs, OBCs and Education)

MEANING OF SOCIAL JUSTICE AND EQUALITY

Social justice and equality have vast social justice dimensions and cover almost everything which promotes the welfare of all the members of the society in general and in particular the welfare of the weaker or backward sections of the society. It implies the following:

(i) Equality of opportunity.
(ii) Economic security.
(iii) Abolition of special privileges of upper sections of society.
(iv) Abolition of social inequality.
(v) Abolition of social evils.
(vi) Protective discrimination, i.e., providing special benefits to backward classes or sections.
(vii) Minimising gaps in wealth.
(viii) Protection of the interest of the workers.
(ix) Fulfilment of basic needs of all the members of society.

SIGNIFICANCE OF SOCIAL JUSTICE AND EQUALITY

Dr. B.R. Ambedkar, the chairman of the drafting committee of the Constitution of India; in his final address to the Constituent Assembly on November 25, 1949, very rightly stressed the importance of social and economic equality in these words:

> "On the social plane, we have in India a society based on the principles of graded inequality which means elevation of some and degradation of other, on the economic plane we have a society in which there are some who have immense wealth as against many who live in abject poverty. On the 26th January 1950, we are going to enter into a life of contradictions. In politics we will have equality and in social and economic life, we will have inequality. In politics, we will be recognising the principle of one man one vote and one vote one value. In our social and economic life, we shall by reason of our social and economic structure, continue to deny the principle of one man one value. How long shall we continue to live this life of contradiction? How long shall we continue to deny equality in our social and economic life? If we continue to deny it for long, we will do so by putting our political democracy in peril. We must remove this contradiction at the earliest possible moment or else those who suffer from inequality will blow up the structure of political democracy."

Social Justice and Equality: Safeguards in the Indian Constitution

Social justice and equality call for a social order in which each member is provided with the maximum opportunities for his optimum development.

Following are the provisions in the Constitution which relate to social justice and equality:

1. Preamble: It *inter alia* mentions

Justice, social, economic and political

Equality of status and opportunity.

2. Fundamental Rights: *Right to Equality*

Article 14: Equality before law.

Article 15: Prohibition of discrimination on grounds of religion, race, caste, sex or place of birth.

Article 16: Equality of opportunity in matters of public appointment.

Article 17: Abolition of untouchability.

Article 29 relates to the protection of the language, script and culture of minorities. It also eliminates discrimination in matters of admission to educational institutions.

3. Directive Principles of State Polity:

Article 38 specifically relates to secure a social order for the promotion of welfare of the people.

Article 38(2) states, "The State shall, in particular, strive to minimise the inequalities in income and endeavour to eliminate inequalities of status, facilities and opportunities."

Article 39 relates to the following:

(a) Right to an adequate means of livelihood.

(b) Checking concentration of wealth in a few hands.

Article 43 and *43(a)* relate to the participation of workers in the management of industries and living wages.

Article 46 relates to the educational and economic interests of SCs, STs and OBCs.

Article 330 relates to reservation of seats for SCs and STs in the Lok Sabha.

Article 331 is concerned with the representation of the Anglo-Indian community in the Lok Sabha.

Article 332 makes reservation of seats for SCs and STs in the Legislative Assemblies of the States.

Article 338 to *342* relate to the appointment of National Commission for SCs, STs and OBCs. Posts have been reserved for various categories.

While discussing the various aspects of equality, it must be remembered that there cannot be 'absolute equality'. Equality implies that the impact of inequality should not result in permanent subordination of some sections of society to others in any of the sphere of socio-economic life.

IMPACT OF SOCIO-ECONOMIC INEQUALITY ON THE INDIAN DEMOCRACY

1. Socio-economic inequality develops social tension which encourages forces of disintegration and thus poses a threat to democracy.
2. On account of socio-economic inequalities, the poor and the weaker sections of the society do not have enough resources to match the resources of the rich, and in this way, financial difficulties create hurdles to contest elections.
3. On account of large resources, the upper classes are able to get more representation in the legislatures.
4. On account of inequalities, the poor and the backward sections tend to lose faith in democratic values.
5. Inequalities tend to turn democracy into autocracy. It negates the principle of equity and justice.
6. Socio-economic inequalities provide handle to the upper classes or the landlords to offer temptations to the backward sections to vote for them.
7. Socio-economic inequalities create discontent and hated among the downtrodden and their fury seeks outlets in riots and violence which vitiate smooth election procedure.

Types of Social and Economic Inequality in India

- Caste inequality *Jati Pratha* Untouchability
- Poverty and income inequality
- Inequality between the rural and urban population
- Gender inequality
- Regional inequality
- Inequality between SCs, STs and other sections
- Inequality in literacy and education

CAUSES OF SOCIAL AND ECONOMIC INEQUALITY

- Untouchability
- Caste system
- Conservative attitude
- Unequal distribution of resources of the community
- Illiteracy
- Colonial legacy
- Gender bias

THREE-FOLD STRATEGY FOR THE EMPOWERMENT OF SCs, STs AND OBCs: MINIMISING INEQUALITY

- Social Empowerment
- Economic Empowerment
- Social Justice

Social Empowerment (Specially Through Education)

Creating an enabling environment for the welfare and development of the socially disadvantaged groups by removing the existing inequalities, disparities and other persisting problems besides providing easy and equal access to basic minimum services through—

- Education being the most effective instrument of empowering the socially disadvantaged groups, all-out efforts to be made to improve the educational status of these groups, especially of women and the girl child.
- Universalisation of primary education by 2007 and at elementary stage by 2010 with a special focus on low literacy pockets, and educationally backward communities, viz. SCs, STs, OBCs, minorities and women with a special focus on the girl child.
- Improving enrolment/retention rates of these groups in schools and thus reducing school drop-out rates through special incentives/support services like hostels, financial assistance, scholarships, free books and food, uniforms, etc. and thus improving the educational status of these groups, especially that of their women and girl children.

- Vocational training/education to improve the technical and productive capabilities of these groups, suiting local needs and market demands.
- Supplementing primary health care services through the Pradhan Mantri Gramodaya Yojana (PMGY) so as to fill the critical gaps, both in the infrastructure and services in the SC/OBC/Minority concentrated areas.
- 'Reaching the Un-reached', viz. SC/OBC/Minority groups, those living in the most backward and neglected areas, in general and their women and the girl children, in particular through the Universalised/ Expanded programmes of ICDS, Supplementary Nutrition Programme, Mid-Day Meals, etc.
- Encouraging the participation of the socially disadvantaged groups in the planning and developmental processes at every level through ensuring their adequate representation in various democratic decision-making institutions like Panchayati Raj/Local Bodies, State Assemblies/Parliament, etc.

Economic Empowerment

The socially disadvantaged groups economically, promotion of employment-cum-income generation activities with an ultimate objective of making them economically independent and self-reliant through:

- Optimising the traditional ability of SCs/OBCs in agricultural production and maximising their productive capacity through endowing a piece of land, upgradation of skills, modern technology, equipment and ensured irrigation facilities.
- Enacting special legislative measures to ensure payment of minimum wages and equal wages with no gender discrimination to the SCs, especially in the informal sector.
- Re-orienting the employment opportunities for the disadvantaged to enable them to face the challenges of

economic reforms and expanding private sector through equipping them suitably with the technical skills and emerging trades.

- Encouraging development of small entrepreneurship through formation of Self-Help Groups and with the support credit and markets through the corporations, exclusively set-up for these Groups.
- Modernisation of technologies and upgradation of skills in traditional arts and crafts sectors such as handlooms, handicrafts, lace making, glass work, metal work, etc. and thus ensuring value addition to the products to compete with the quality of the products of modern markets.
- Motivating the private and corporate sectors to invest in the welfare and development of weaker sections and thus fulfil their social obligations/responsibilities.

Social Justice

Eliminating all types of discrimination against the socially disadvantaged groups with the strength of legislative support, affirmative action, awareness generation/conscientiousness of the target groups, and change in the mind-set of the people through:

Reservation Policy: Strict implementation of reservation policy in education and services for SCs and in services for OBCs.

Eradication of Manual Scavenging: Total eradication of the most inhuman practice of manual scavenging continuing still in the present-day civilised world on a time-bound basis and with a Mission Mode Approach by 2007, by conversion of dry latrines into wet and weaning away the manual scavengers from this profession and rehabilitate them with alternative attractive and sustainable jobs.

Safeguards Against Atrocities: To uphold civil rights and prevent/curb social discrimination, exploitation, untouchability and atrocities against the disadvantaged groups through effective legislations.

Establishment of Mobile Courts: To set-up adequate number of special/mobile Courts in each District for speedy settlement/

redressal of grievances for these groups and extend timely and adequate financial support as a measure of social justice to compensate/rehabilitate the victims.

Strengthening the Working of Commissions: Revitalising the four already existing Statutory Commissions, viz. for SCs and STs, for OBCs, for minorities, and for safai karamcharis and thus make them effective instruments to safeguard the rights and interests of these groups and thus ensure social justice to them.

Organising Awareness Programmes: Special 3-pronged strategy of 'Awareness Generation'—through changing the mindset and attitudes of the people towards these groups; 'Conscientiousness of the Target Groups'—to make them conscious of their own rights, privileges and governmental support available for them; 'Sensitising both officials and non-officials'—with special training programmes so that they can work with right perspective to meet the special needs of these groups.

SCHEDULED CASTES AND SCHEDULED TRIBES: SOCIAL JUSTICE AND EQUALITY

Meaning of Scheduled Castes and Scheduled Tribes

There is no set definition of SCs and STs but under Article 341 and Article 342 of the Constitution, certain classes are declared as SCs and STs.

Population of Scheduled Castes

In 2001, the population of Scheduled castes was 166.6 million, which accounted for 16.2 per cent of the total population.

Almost half of the total population of SC is concentrated in the states of Bihar, Haryana, Madhya Pradesh, Punjab, Rajasthan and U.P.—popularly known as Hindi belt in the north.

In the south, SCs are concentrated mainly in Andhra Pradesh and Tamil Nadu.

In the east, they are in Bengal and in the west in Maharashtra.

Traditionally Considered Characteristics of STs

1. Very little education.
2. Livelihood dependent upon land.
3. Very poor.

Social Life: Tribal people at different places have different cultures, faiths, traditions and values.

Scheduled Tribes

Origin of the Term Scheduled Tribes (ST): As distinct from the so-called mainstream population, the British used this term with respect to groups living in forests and hills, etc. It was also used with the prefix like indigenous people, etc. The term Scheduled Tribe denotes people belonging to these groups. Traditionally they have had very little contact with the main culture.

Traditionally Considered Characteristics of the Tribal People

1. The tribal people live in rather inaccessible parts of the country.
2. The tribal people live away from the civilised world.
3. They belong to these races—Australoid or Mongoloids or Negrito.
4. They speak tribal dialects.
5. They believe in ghosts and spirits and worship them.
6. They profess primitive religion known as 'Animism'.
7. Their chief occupations are gathering forest products, hunting, etc.
8. They are, by and large, meat eaters.

Total Tribal Population

The population of tribal people in 2001 was estimated to have reached 84.3 million. This represented 8.19 per cent of country's total population.

Population Profile of the Tribal People

1. The largest concentration of ST population is found in the North-Eastern States: Mizoram (94.8%); Nagaland (87.7%); Meghalaya (85.5%); and Arunachal Pradesh (63.7%).
2. Union Territories: Lakshadweep (93.2%); Dadra and Nagar Haveli (79%); Andaman and Nicobar Islands (5.5%).
3. Madhya Pradesh (23.3%); Orissa (22.2%); Rajasthan (12.4%); Maharashtra (9.3%); Bihar (7.7%).
4. Almost nil in Haryana, Punjab, Chandigarh, Delhi and Pondicherry.

Table 4.1: Total Population, Sex-wise and Residence-wise (2001) of SC, ST

	Total Population of India	*SC*	*ST*
	1,028,610,328	166,635,700	84,326,240
Males	532,156,772	86,088,760	42,640,829
Females	496,453,556	80,546,940	41,685,411

Note: India (Excluding the population of Mao-Maram, Paomata and Purural Sub-division of Senapati District of Manipur.
('Census of India 2001': Final Population Totals) (Registrar General & Census Commissioner India, 2004)

Table 4.2: Specific Articles in the Constitution for SCs and STs

Sl. No.	*Article*	*Main Provisions*
1.	Article 15(2)	Removal of any disability, liability, restriction or conditions with regard to access to shops, public restaurants, hotels and places of public entertainment or use of wells, tanks, bathing ghats, roads and places of public resort maintained wholly or partially out of state funds or dedicated to the use of general public.

(*Contd.*)

Sl. No.	*Article*	*Main Provisions*
2.	Article 16 (4 and 4A) and 335	Permitting the State to make reservation for backward classes in public services in case of inadequate representations and requiring the State to consider claims of the Scheduled Castes and Scheduled Tribes in the making of appointments to public services.
3.	Article 17	Abolition of untouchability and forbid-dding its practice in any form.
4.	Article 19 (e)	General right of all citizens to move freely, settle in and acquire property in any part of the country.
5.	Article 25 (b)	Providing for social welfare and throwing open by law of Hindu religious institu-tions of public character to all classes and sections of Hindus.
6.	Article 46	It enjoins upon the state to promote with special care the educational and economic interests of the weaker sections of the society and in particular of the SCs and the STs and promises to protect them from social injustice and all forms of exploit-tation.
7.	Article 164 (1)	It provides for the appointment of Special Minister in some States for looking after the work of SCs and STs.
8.	Article 244, 244A, and 275 (1)	Special provision for administration and control of scheduled and tribal areas in some states.

MEASURES FOR THE DEVELOPMENT OF SCs AND STs

1. Acts Passed for the Protection of SCs and STs

A. *Legislation Against Untouchability (1955) and Protection of Civil Rights Act (1976)*

For enlarging the scope and making penal provisions more stringent, the Untouchability (Offences) Act, 1955 has been comprehensively amended and renamed as the Protection of Civil Rights Act, 1955 which came into force with effect from November 19, 1976. This Act provides for penalties for preventing any person on grounds of untouchability, from enjoying the rights accruing on account of abolition of untouchability.

B. *Legislation to Check Atrocities Against SCs and STs*

Scheduled Castes and Scheduled Tribes (Prevention of Atrocities) Act, 1989, which came into force on January 30, 1990, specifies offences which are considered as atrocities and provides for deterrent punishments for commission of the same. It also envisages preventive measures, and states to evolve schemes, among others, for economic and social rehabilitation of such victims. All States and Union Territories except Arunachal Pradesh and Nagaland have specified special courts for trial of offences under this Act. Exclusive special courts have been set up in Andhra Pradesh, Madhya Pradesh, Rajasthan, Gujarat and Karnataka.

2. National Commission for SCs and STs

In 1990, by the 65th Amendment of the Constitution, the Special Officer's post under Article 338 has been substituted by the National Commission for Scheduled Castes and Scheduled Tribes. The Commission suggests measures for the upliftment of SCs and STs.

3. Parliamentary Committees

Government had set up three Parliamentary Committees, first in 1966, second in 1971 and third in 1973 to examine the implementation of the constitutional safeguards for welfare of Scheduled Castes and Scheduled Tribes. The Committee has since then constituted as a Standing Committee of Parliament on Labour and Welfare.

APPROACH FOR EMPOWERING TRIBALS

- *Resolving the Un-resolved Issues through*:
  - Taking effective steps to prevent the serious problem of displacement of tribals and ensuring their effective rehabilitation through a laid down Rehabilitation Policy.
  - Involving tribals, especially those engaged in shifting cultivation, closely and gainfully in joint forest management, social forestry, agro forestry, etc. and facilitate rightful collection and gainful disposal of minor forest produce (MFP) and other produce.
  - Strengthening the grassroot democratic institutions, viz. Gram Sabhas, etc.
- *Solving the Persisting Problems through*:
  - Providing basic minimum services, viz. food, nutrition, safe drinking water, primary health care, education, safe environment, productive assets at least at the level of survival and sustenance with a special focus on women and children.
  - Promoting educational development among the tribals especially through reducing dropout rates and encouraging enrolment/retention with a special focus on women and the girl child.
  - Making education relevant and suitable to their milieu, local situations and functional needs besides vocationalisation of education to equip the tribal youth with the most wanted technical knowledge and upgradation of skills.
  - Developing Forest Villages, on priority basis, by ensuring basic infrastructure and with basic minimum services for those tribals living therein.
  - Review and reform of the working of the financial and other support mechanisms.
  - Effective implementation of the Indian Penal Code.

- *Enactment of the Scheduled Tribes and Other Traditional Forest Dwellers (Recognition of Forest Rights) Act, 2006*
  - Aims to improve the lives of the tribals and other traditional forest dwellers living in forest by vesting the right to self-cultivation of forest land for livelihood, right of ownership, collection, use and disposal of minor forest produce, traditional and customary rights; Rules for carrying out the provisions of the Act are being framed and shall be notified shortly.
- *New Scheme of "Top Class Education for ST Students" introduced from 2007-08*
  - To encourage meritorious ST students for pursuing studies at degree and post degree level in any selected Government or private institutes covering fields of management, medicine, engineering, law and commercial courses.
  - 635 scholarship per year to be awarded to cover full tuition fee and other non-refundable dues in respect of Government/Government funded institution; for private institution with a ceiling of Rs.2 lakh per annum per student,; and Rs.3.72 lakh per student for the private sector flying clubs for Commercial Training.

National Commission For Safai Karamcharis Act, 1993

Composition of the Commission: Under this Act, the Commission shall consist of:

(a) a Chairperson
(b) a Vice-chairperson
(c) Five members

One of the members to be a woman.

Functions and Powers of the Commission

The Commission shall perform all or any of the following functions, namely:

(a) recommend to the Central Government specific programmes of action toward elimination of inequalities in status, facilities and opportunities for Safai Karamcharis under a time-bound action plan;

(b) study and evaluate the implementation of the programmes and schemes relating to the social and economic rehabilitation of Safai Karamcharis and make recommendations to the Central Government and State Governments for better coordination and implementation of such programmes and schemes;

(c) investigate specific grievances and take *suo motu* notice of matters relating to non-implementation of—

   (i) programmes or schemes in respect of any group of Safai Karamcharis;

   (ii) decisions, guidelines or instructions, aimed at mitigating the hardship of Safai Karamcharis;

   (iii) measures for the social and economic upliftment of Safai Karamcharis;

   (iv) the provisions of any law in it application to Safai Karamcharis.

OVERALL STRATEGIES FOR THE DEVELOPMENT AND WELFARE OF THE SCs AND STs

The Government has adopted the following fourteen-fold strategy for the development of the Scheduled Castes and Scheduled Tribes:

1. Specific provisions in the Constitution for the advancement of SCs and STs.
2. Special Component Plans formed by the Central and State Government for the development of SCs and STs.

3. Special Central Assistance to the States for the projects taken up by the State Governments for the welfare of the SCs and STs.
4. Setting up Scheduled Caste Development Corporation (SCDCs) and ST Development Corporation.
5. Legislative measures.
6. Reservation of seats in the Parliament and State Legislatures.
7. Reservation in services.
8. Constitution of National Commission.
9. Assistance to voluntary organisations for Scheduled Castes and Scheduled Tribes.

DIRECTIONS CONTAINED IN NATIONAL POLICY ON EDUCATION (1986 AND 1992) ON THE EDUCATION OF THE SCHEDULED CASTES

4.4 The central focus in the SCs' educational development is their equalisation with the non-SC population at all stages and levels of education, in all areas and in all the four dimensions – rural male, rural female, urban male and urban female.

4.5 The measures contemplated for this purpose include:

(i) Incentives to indigent families to send their children to school regularly till they reach the age of 14;

(ii) Pre-matric Scholarship scheme for children of families engaged in occupations, such as, scavenging etc. to be made applicable from Class I onwards. All children of such families, regardless of incomes, will be covered by this scheme and time-bound programmes targeted on them will be undertaken;

(iii) Constant micro-planning and verification to ensure that the enrolment, retention and successful completion of courses by SC, and provision of remedial courses to improve their prospects for further education and in employment;

(iv) The recruitment of teachers from Scheduled Castes;

(v) Provision of facilities for SC students in hostels at district headquarters, according to a phased programme;

(vi) Location of school buildings, balwadis and Adult Education Centres in such a way as to facilitate full participation of the Scheduled Castes.

4.5 *Revised Para* of Education Policy, 1992 (vii) The utilisation of Jawahar Rozgar Yojana resources so as to make substantial educational facilities available to the Scheduled Castes; and

4.5 *NPE 1986 Para* (vii) the utilisation of N.R.E.P. and R.L.E.G.P. resources so as to make substantial educational facilities available to the Scheduled Castes;

(viii) Constant innovation in finding new methods to increase the participation of the Scheduled Castes in the educational process.

The Education of Scheduled Tribes

4.6 The following measures will be taken urgently to bring the Scheduled Tribes on par with others:

4.6 [*Revised Para* (i)] Priority will be accorded to opening primary schools in tribal areas. The construction of school buildings will be undertaken in these areas on a priority basis under the normal funds for education, as well as under the Jawahar Rozgar Yojana, Tribal Welfare Schemes, etc.

4.6 [*NPE 1986 Para* (i)] Priority will be accorded to opening primary schools in tribal areas. The construction of school buildings will be undertaken in these areas on a priority basis under the normal funds for education, as well as under the N.R.E.P., R.L.E.G.P., Tribal Welfare Schemes, etc.

(ii) The socio-cultural milieu of the ST has its distinctive characteristics including, in many cases, their own spoken languages. This underlines the need to develop the curricula and devise institutional materials in tribal languages at the initial stages, with arrangements for switching over to the regional languages.

(iii) Educated and promising Scheduled Tribe youths are encouraged and trained to take up teaching in tribal areas.
(iv) Residential schools, including Ashram Schools will be established on a large scale.
(v) Incentive schemes will be formulated for the Scheduled Tribes, keeping in view their special needs and life styles. Scholarships for higher education will emphasise technical, professional and para-professional courses. Special remedial courses and other programmes to remove psycho-social impediments will be provided to improve their performance in various courses.
(vi) Anganwadis, Non-formal and Adult Education Centres will be opened on a priority basis in areas predominantly inhabited by the Scheduled Tribes.
(vii) The curriculum at all stages of education will be designed to create an awareness of the rich cultural identity of the tribal people as also of their enormous creative talent.

MEASURES BEING TAKEN TO PROMOTE EDUCATION AMONG SCs: EQUALISATION WITH NON-SCs

The central focus in the SCs' educational development is their equalisation with the non-SC population at all stages and levels of education, in all areas and in all the four dimensions-rural male, rural female, urban male and urban female. The measures being taken as per directions given in NPE.

Promotion of Education Among STs

The measures are being taken to bring the Scheduled Tribes on par with others as per directions in NPE.

Preparatory Classes and Compensatory Instruction for SCs and STs

Many children belonging to the Scheduled Castes, Scheduled Tribes and economically weaker sections come from a comparatively poor environment. They may not be neat or smart. Their usage of standard language may be poor. Their vocabulary is underdeveloped as compared to their peers. They may not have formed the initial mathematical concepts. On the other hand they may be more enthusiastic to learn. Because of the lack of a congenial home environment, these children may not be in a position to complete their home assignments. Their parents are usually employed as landless labour or in other manual or agrarian activities. Therefore, such children are not able to conceptualise their future as educated persons.

There is the need to conduct some preparatory classes for children coming from the Scheduled Castes and Scheduled Tribes. The primary objective of conducting such classes is to raise the school entry ability level of such children. This is also helpful in having a somewhat homogeneous grouping in the class. The classes may be conducted two to three weeks in advance of the general admissions. Classes may be conducted on healthy habits, personal and environmental cleanliness, eating habits etc. The children may also be helped in improving the pronunciation of the words and picking up standard language. For this, they may be motivated to participate in discussions, recitation and story-telling etc. Initial concepts of mathematics may also be introduced.

Remedial Instruction

Students coming from Scheduled Castes and Scheduled Tribes are also likely to be deficient in the scholastic areas. The school may provide some remedial education programmes. Adoption of instructional strategies, such as peer group learning, monitorial assistance, diagnostic testing and tutoring would help to improve the educational levels of these learners.

Provision of outdoor games and activities, co-curricular and work experience activities will also help in the retention of such children in the schools and create an interest in them for continuing schooling.

ROLE OF THE TEACHERS

The teachers can play an important role in developing a

favourable school climate conducive to the educational progress of Scheduled Castes and Scheduled Tribes. Some suggestions in this regard are given here.

1. The teacher's own example in his behaviour towards students belonging to these castes is the most effective and powerful way to build up a congenial climate.
2. The school staff should ensure non-discrimination between the children of Scheduled Castes, Scheduled Tribes and other communities.
3. The school staff should avoid the use of the caste names or derogatory words while calling roll calls or naming children.
4. Teachers should provide equal opportunities to all the children to participate in the curricular and co-curricular activities of the school, including games.
5. Frequent meetings between the staff, school teachers and parents of Scheduled Castes and Scheduled Tribes children should be arranged. The details of the schemes for promoting education amongst Scheduled Castes and Scheduled Tribes should be explained to the parents at these meetings. It should be impressed upon them that they must continue the education of their children.
6. Special attention should be paid to motivating parents to educate girls.
7. Teachers should suggest to illiterate parents the advantages gained by attending functional literacy classes in the centre.

OTHER BACKWARD CLASSES (OBCs)

Constitutional Provisions

1. *Article 15(4) of the Constitution*: It enjoins upon the state the creation of special provisions for the advancement of any socially and educationally backward classes of citizens or for the Scheduled Castes and Scheduled Tribes.

2. *Article 16(4)*: It enables the State for making provisions for the reservation of appointments or posts in favour of any backward class of citizens which in the opinion of the state is not adequately represented in the services under the state.

3. *Article 38*: It makes it obligatory for the state to "strive to promote the welfare of the people by securing and protecting as effectively as it may a social order, in which Justice, Social, Economic and Political shall form all the institutions of the national life."

4. *Article 46*: It contains a very significant directive regarding promotion of educational and economic interests of other weaker sections and protecting them from social injustice and all forms of exploitation.

5. *Part XVI of the Constitution*: It contains "special provisions relating to certain classes" and under this part, Article 340 envisages the appointment of a Commission to investigate the conditions of Backward Classes.

Mandal Commission (1978-1980)

Appointment of the Mandal Commission

In pursuance of the Article 340 of the Constitution of India regarding the appointment of a Commission for the promotion of the Backward Classes, the President of India appointed a Commission under the Chairmanship of B.P. Mandal in 1978.

Major Recommendations

The Commission in its report, submitted in 1980, made the following recommendations:

1. Twenty-seven per cent of the posts in public services should be reserved for Other Backward Classes (OBCs).
2. Welfare programmes specially for the OBCs should be started by the Government of India in the same manner and to the same extent already done in the case of Scheduled Castes and Scheduled Tribes.

3. Special educational schemes with emphasis on vocational training should be started for OBCs.
4. Seats should be reserved for OBC students in all scientific, technical and professional institutions run by the Centre as well as the State Governments.

By and large, all the recommendations have been accepted. Only the 'creamy layer' (upper section of OBCs) has been excluded from the benefits.

National Commission for Backward Classes

The process of identifying the OBC is an unending process and is kept open. The government also set up on August 14, 1993, a National Commission for Backward Classes as a permanent body for entertaining, examining and recommending upon requests for inclusion and complaints of under-inclusion in the lists of OBC class citizens.

National Backward Classes Finance and Development Corporation

This body was set up by the Government of India in January 1992 as a company with the objective of providing concessional loans to the members of backward classes living below the poverty line. The Corporation has also launched a special scheme for eligible women beneficiaries of backward classes under the name of SWARNIMA.

Educational Schemes for the Welfare of OBCs

From 1998-99, following schemes have been launched for the welfare of OBCs:

(a) Pre-examination coaching; to coach candidates belonging to OBCs whose parent's/guardian's annual income is less than Rs. one lakh,
(b) Hostels for OBC Boys and Girls,
(c) Pre-matric Scholarships,
(d) Post-matric Scholarships,

(e) Assistance to voluntary organisations: The scheme involves the voluntary sector to improve educational and socio-economic conditions of the OBCs to get them gainfully employed.

Summing up: Educational Provisions for the Deprived Sections: Equality of Educational Opportunity

It is observed that well-planned, sustained and vigorous efforts as stated below would go a long way in promoting education among the deprived sections:

1. Promotion of mother-tongue as the medium of instruction.
2. Need based curriculum.
3. Special training of teachers.
4. Provision of suitable school building/accommodation.
5. Extension of Ashram schools.
6. Provision of extensive facilities.
7. Encouragement of tribal parents.
8. Flexibility in school hours.
9. Popularisation of tribal dialects.
10. Economic incentives to parents.
11. Special training for talented tribal students.
12. Provision of audio-visual aids.
13. Improvement of teacher-community relations.
14. Relaxation of prescribed norms for the opening of schools in tribal areas.
15. Opening of non-formal education centres.
16. Incentive programme for adult education.
17. Relaxation of prescribed pupil-teacher ratio.
18. Guidance facilities.
19. Incentives for students.
20. Provision of scholarships.
21. Organisation of study camps.
22. New initiatives for universalisation of elementary education.

23. Facilities for teachers – incentives like reservation of seats for their wards in Public Schools, Sainik Schools, etc.
24. Conducive environment in educational institutions.
25. Educational provisions – teaching-learning material.
26. Preparatory classes.
27. Compensatory and remedial teaching.
28. Relaxation of qualifications for tribal people in teacher training.
29. Effective monitoring programme.
30. Special role of the teachers.

For the successful working of Indian democracy and the achievement of national objectives as contained in the Constitution, it is very important to take speedy measures for the promotion of education among the children of the weaker sections.

GRADUAL INCREASE IN LITERACY RATES AMONG SCs AND STs

The literacy percentage of Scheduled Castes increased from 10.7 in 1961 to 54.69 in 2001. The literacy among males was 16.96 per cent in 1961, which increased by 49.68 percentage points and reached 66.64 per cent in 2001. The literacy of Scheduled Caste females was as low as 3.29 per cent during 1961, which was now increased to 41.90 per cent thereby registering in increase of 38.61 percentage points during 1961-2001. The literacy of Scheduled Tribes was 8.53 per cent during 1961, which has increased to 47.10 per cent in 2001. In the year 1961 the literacy percentage of Scheduled Tribe Males was 13.83 per cent, which increased to 59.17 per cent in the year 2001. The literacy percentage of Scheduled Tribe females, which was as low as 3.16 per cent during 1961, increased to 34.76 per cent in the year 2001. A comparative position of literacy percentages of Scheduled Castes and Scheduled Tribes in Rural-Urban areas is given below in Statement.

Literacy Rates of SC/ST by Sex and Urban/Rural, 1961 to 2001

Year/Region	*Scheduled Castes*			*Scheduled Tribes*		
	Male	*Female*	*Persons*	*Male*	*Female*	*Persons*
1961						
Rural	15.06	2.52	8.89	13.37	2.90	8.16
Urban	32.21	10.04	21.81	30.43	13.45	22.41
Total	**16.96**	**3.29**	**10.27**	**13.83**	**3.16**	**8.53**
1971						
Rural	20.04	5.06	12.77	16.92	4.36	10.68
Urban	38.93	16.99	28.65	37.09	19.64	28.84
Total	**22.36**	**6.44**	**14.67**	**17.63**	**4.85**	**11.30**
1981						
Rural	27.91	8.45	18.48	22.94	6.81	14.92
Urban	47.54	24.34	36.60	47.60	27.32	37.93
Total	**31.12**	**10.93**	**21.38**	**24.52**	**8.04**	**16.35**
1991						
Rural	45.95	19.45	33.25	38.45	16.02	27.38
Urban	66.60	42.29	55.11	66.56	45.66	56.60
Total	**49.91**	**23.76**	**37.41**	**40.65**	**18.19**	**29.60**
2001						
Rural	63.66	37.84	51.16	57.39	32.44	45.02
Urban	77.93	57.49	68.12	77.77	59.87	69.09
Total	**66.64**	**41.90**	**54.69**	**59.17**	**34.76**	**47.10**

Source: *Educational Statistics 2005-2006*, Department of Education, Government of India.

5

Education for Secularism, Democracy and Socialism

ORIGIN AND MEANING OF THE TERM SECULARISM

The word 'Secularism' was first used in 1846 by a British thinker George Holydake (1817-1906). In his book '*English Secularism*', he defined secularism as, "Secularism is a code of duty pertaining to this life, founded on considerations purely human and intended mainly for those who find theology, indefinite or inadequate, unreliable or unbelievable."

Holydake based secularism as a social and ethical system, on the following principles:

1. Principle of material and cultural improvement of human beings.
2. Principle of respect and research of all truth, whatever be its source.
3. Principle of concern for 'this present age' or world and its improvement.
4. Principle of independent rational morality, which does not base itself on faith in divine order commandment.

The meaning attached to secularism tends to minimise the importance of the spirit and the Divine power. It also tends to ignore the spiritual side. Both the elements are considered basic to Indian thinkers. The definition lays stress on material improvement only.

The word 'Secularism' is derived from the Latin word '*Saeculum*' meaning 'this present age'. Accordingly Holydake also emphasised the word 'this age'.

The Dictionary meaning of 'Secularism' are as under:

(1) '*Chamber's Dictionary*': "The belief that the state, moral education, etc. should be independent of religion."

(2) '*Oxford Dictionary*': "The doctrine that morality should be based solely in regard to the well-being of mankind in the present life, to the exclusion of all considerations drawn from belief in God."

(3) '*Webster's Dictionary*': "A system of doctrines and practices that rejects any form of religious faith and worship."

(4) As explained in *Wikipedia,* the term connotes;... 'that certain practices or institutions should exist separately from religion or religious belief'; '... it asserts the right to be free from religious rule and teachings, and freedom from government imposition of religion upon the people, within a state that is neutral on matters of belief, and gives no state privileges or subsidies to religions'; '... it refers to a belief that human activities and decisions, especially political ones, should be based on evidence and fact rather than religious influence'; '... in European laicism, it has been argued that secularism is a movement towards modernisation, and away from traditional religious values'; '.... In United States, some argue that state secularism has served to a greater extent to protect religion from governmental interference, while secularism on a social scale is less prevalent'; '... within countries as well, differing political movements support secularism for varying reasons'; '... in political terms, secularism is a movement towards the separation of religion and government'; '... secularism can also be the social ideology in which religion and supernatural beliefs are not seen as the key to understanding the world and are instead segregated from matters of governance and reasoning... and in this sense, secularism can be involved in the promotion of science, reason, and naturalistic thinking'.

SECULARISM IN THE INDIAN CONSTITUTION

The term 'Secularism' did not occur in the Constitution of India when it was adopted in 1950. It was inserted in the Constitution of India in 1976 as it was feared that religious fundamentalism was on the increase and it was posing a great threat to national unity and integrity.

Following are the provisions on Secularism in the Constitution:

1. *Article 15: Prohibition of Discrimination on Grounds of Religion, Race, Caste, Sex or Place of Birth.* (i) The State shall not discriminate against any citizen on grounds only of religion, race, caste, sex, place of birth or any of them, (ii) No citizen on grounds only of religion, race, sex, place of birth shall be denied access to shops, wells, tanks, etc.

2. *Article 25(1): Freedom of Conscience*: According to this Article, all citizens are equally entitled to freedom of conscience and the right to profess, practice and propagate religion. However, while the freedom of conscience is absolute, i.e., without any restriction, the exercise of freedom of propagation of religion is subject to restrictions in the interest of harmony, public morality and order.

3. *Article 27: Exemption from the Payment of Taxes.* As per this Article, no person shall be compelled to pay any taxes, the proceeds of which are specifically appropriated in payment of expenses for the promotion or maintenance of any particular religion or religious denomination.

Views of Great Thinkers on Secularism

1. *H.V. Kamat*, a veteran Parliamentarian expanded the concept of secularism in the Constituent Assembly as "When I say that State should not identify itself with any particular religion, I do not mean to say that a State should be anti-religious or irreligious. We have certainly declared India to be a secular state. But to my mind, a secular state is neither a Godless state, nor an irreligious or an anti-religious State. In

short, by a secular State is meant that the State shall not make any discrimination whatsoever on the ground of religion or community against a person professing any particular form of religious faith. This means that no particular religion in the State will receive any patronage or protection."

2. *Dr. B.R. Ambedkar,* the principal architect of our Constitution explains secularism in the following words, "Secular State does not mean that it shall not take into consideration the religious sentiments of the people. All that Secular State means is, that this Parliament shall not be competent to impose any particular religion upon the rest of the people. This is the only limitation that the Constitution recognises. (Parliamentary Debates, 1951 Vol. III, Part-II)."

3. *Dr. Rajendra Prasad, the first President of India* has very clearly observed that becoming secular, India has not been anti-religious or irreligious. He stated, "There are some who think that because we are a Secular State, we do not believe in religion or spiritual values. Far from being so, it really means that in this country all are free to profess or preach the faith of their liking and that we wish well of all religions and want than to develop in their own way without any hindrance."

4. *Dr. Radhakrishnan, the second President of India* explained secularism as follows:

"When India is said to be a secular state, it does not mean that we reject the reality of an unseen spirit or the relevance of religion to life or that we exalt irreligion. It does not mean that secularism itself becomes a positive religion or that the State assumes divine prerogatives. Though faith in the Supreme is the basic principle of the Indian traditions, the Indian state will not identify itself with or controlled by any particular religion. We hold that no one religion should be given preferential status, or unique distinction, that no one religion would be accorded special privileges in national life or international relations for that would be a violation of the basic principles of democracy and contrary to the best interest of religion and government. This view of religious impartiality, or comprehension and forbearance, has a prophetic role to play within the national and the international life."

5. *Jawaharlal Nehru, the first Prime Minister of India* has explained the secular nature of our State. "It means while religion is completely free, the state including in its wide fold various religions and cultures, gives protection and opportunities to all and thus, brings about an atmosphere of tolerance and cooperation."

6. On the concept of a 'Secular State', *Justice M.H. Beg,* in his judgement in *Ziyauddin Burhamudin Bukhari vs. Brijmohan Ramdass Mehra and Bros.* (1975 Suppl. S.C.R. 281) said:

"The secular state, rising above all differences of religion, attempts to secure the good of all its citizens irrespective of their religious beliefs and practices. It is neutral or impartial in extending its benefits to citizens of all castes and creeds. Maitland has pointed out that such a state has to ensure, through its laws that the existence or exercise of political or civil right or the right or capacity to occupy any office or position under it or to perform any public duty connected with it does not depend upon the profession or practice of any particular religion.

Our Constitution and the laws framed thereunder leave citizens free to work out happy and harmonious relationships between their religious and the quite separable secular fields of law and politics. But they do not permit an unjustifiable invasion of what belongs to one sphere by what pertains really to another. It is for courts to determine, in a case of dispute, whether any sphere was or was not properly interfered with, in accordance with the Constitution, even by a purported law."

In the *Kesvananda Bharti case* (AIR 1973 SC 1461), secularism was held to be a purported law."

7. In the *Ayodhya case* (AIR 1995 SC 605), the Supreme Court explained secularism thus:

"It is clear from the constitutional scheme that it guarantees equality in the matter of religion to all individuals and groups irrespective of their faith emphasising that there is no religion of the State itself. The Preamble of the Constitution read in particular with articles 25 to 28 emphasises this aspect and indicates that it is in this manner the concept of secularism embodied in the constitutional scheme as a creed adopted by the Indian people has to be understood while examining the constitutional validity of any legislation on the touch-stone of the Constitution. The concept of secularism is one facet of the right to equality woven as the central golden thread in the fabric depicting the pattern of the scheme in our Constitution."

INDIAN CONCEPT OF SECULARISM AND A SECULAR STATE

The Indian concept of secularism is expressed in the following often quoted principles:

1. *'Sarva-dharma-samantva'* or *'Sarva-dharma-sambhava'*—equal regard for all faiths and creeds.
2. *'Ekam Brahma Vipra Bahuda Vadanti'*—God is one, wise men call Him by different names.

Although the word secularism was introduced only in 1976 in our Constitution, our secularism is historical. We have had great breadth of vision as expressed above.

Ashoka's secular outlook is one of the landmarks not only of Indian civilisation but also of the human civilisation. He made a passionate appeal for developing a spirit of reverence and tolerance for all faiths.

India as a Secular State. Ours is a secular State. It means that the State shall not discriminate against the followers of a particular religion. All Indians—Hindus, Muslims, Sikhs, Christians and others have the freedom to practise their religion.

Characteristics of the Secular State of India

1. Indian State treats all religions on equal footing.
2. Indian State neither interferes with nor promotes any religion.

3. It permits individual and collective freedom of religion to all citizens.
4. It views all individuals as citizens with equal rights and not as members of any particular religious group.
5. It is not against any religion.
6. It functions in a way independent of religion.
7. It allows religious education in some educational institutions run and managed by minorities subject to certain conditions.

Secular Outlook or Characteristics of a Secular-Minded Individual

Following salient features of secularism emerge from the above stated views:

1. Secular outlook treats all religion on an equal footing.
2. Secular outlook accepts freedom of religion.
3. Secular outlook implies freedom of worship.
4. Secular outlook implies tolerance.
5. Secular outlook encourages rational thinking.
6. Secular outlook views all citizens with equal rights.
7. Secular outlook encourages moral and spiritual values.
8. Secular outlook believes in co-existence.
9. Secular outlook stresses free inquiry.
10. Secular outlook means freedom of mind from dogmatic ideas.
11. Secular outlook is not a negation of religion.

EDUCATIONAL IMPLICATIONS OF SECULARISM

Secular education should be imparted in educational institutions for the following reasons:

1. Secular education develops a moral outlook.
2. Secular education helps in the development of liberal attitudes and values.

3. Secular education develops wider-vision.
4. Secular education develops an attitude of appreciation and understanding of others' point of view.
5. Secular education develops democratic values.
6. Secular education develops scientific temper of mind.
7. Secular education develops humanistic outlook.
8. Secular education synthesises materialism and spiritualism.
9. Secular education serves as an antidote to religious fanaticism and hatred.

Secularism and Different Dimensions of Education

Educational Aims: These include development of a wider outlook, moral outlook, rational attitude, scientific temper and love for humanity.

Curriculum: Curriculum to include contents, values and experiences conducive to the above mentioned aim. Lives of great personalities to be included. Celebration of festivals of different faiths to be organised.

Recognition of Educational Institutions: Only those educational institutions to be recognised which follow secular values.

Limitations of Secularism

One of the most glaring limitations is that the word secular has different interpretation. Its meaning are not clarified in the Constitution. It means different things to different people.

Summing up: Secularism accords an important places to ethical, moral and spiritual values. These must be inculcated in the students through education.

Secular outlook should be given in the contents of textbooks.

The teacher should not discriminate students on the basis of religion or belief.

Admission should be given to students irrespective of religious belief.

DEMOCRACY AND EDUCATION

Meaning of Democracy

At the outset, it may be emphasised that democracy is a way of life and not only a political system.

In view of the respect for the dignity of the individual and his full development, it is felt that democracy is the only instrument for the achievement of this objective.

The word democracy is derived from two Greek words, *demos* or *demose* meaning 'people' and *Kratein* or *kratia* meaning 'rule'. Thus it implies the 'rule of the people'.

Definitions of Democracy

There is no exaggeration when it is stated that there are as many definitions as there are thinkers.

E.B. Burns in his *Ideas in Conflict* (1960) observed, "Few words have been more loosely and variously defined than democracy. It has almost literally meant all things to all men."

Here some of the most acceptable definitions of democracy are given.

1. The Greek philosopher *Cleon* defined democracy in 422 B.C. in these words, "That shall be democracy which shall be of the people, by the people, for the people."
2. *Aristotle* (384-322 B.C.) defined democracy as 'a government of many'.
3. *U.S. President, Abraham Lincoln* (1809-65) defined democracy "as the government of the people, by the people and for the people."
4. *Lord Brycc* (1832-1932), a British jurist, historian and diplomat gave a functional definition of democracy in these words. "The word democracy denotes that form

of government in which the ruling power of the state is legally vested, not in any particular class or classes, but in the members of the community as a whole. This means, in communities which act by voting, that rule belongs to the majority as no other method has been found for determining peacefully and legally which is deemed to be the will of the community."

5. *Bassett* defines democracy as, "It is a political system by which every citizen has an opportunity of participating through discussion in an attempt to reach voluntary agreement as to what shall be done for the good of the community as a whole."
6. *Sir John Seeley* defines democracy as "government in which everyone has a share."
7. According to *Barker*, "Democracy is a mode of spirit and an attitude of the mind."
8. *Gattell* writes, "Democracy is that form of government in which the mass of the population possesses the right to share in the exercise of sovereign power."
9. According to former U.S. President, *F.D. Roosevelt* (1882-1945), "Democracy is not a mere matter of universal suffrage and unhampered expression of the people's will. It must be a positive and constructive force in the daily lives of the people and provide not merely for political but economic needs also. If men were forced to choose between liberty and bread, they would choose bread."
10. A very suitable definition of democracy is also found in the words of the University Education Commission (1948-49). "Democracy is a way of life and not merely a political arrangement. It is based on the principle of equal freedom and equal right for its members, regardless of race, religion, sex, occupation or economic status."

Factors Leading to the Development of Modern Democracy

Modern democracy got an impetus from five events which are termed as 'great revolutions'. These are:

(i) The Glorious Revolution, 1688 (England).
(ii) The American Revolution, 1776.
(iii) The French Revolution, 1789.
(iv) The Industrial Revolution, (eighteenth and nineteenth centuries).
(v) The Russian Revolution, 1917. However, this was confined to the supremacy and involvement of the working class. It was basically a form of economic democracy.

SIGNIFICANCE OF EACH LETTER IN THE TERM DEMOCRACY: VALUES OF DEMOCRACY

The spirit of democracy as a way of life and a form of government may be explained by assigning ideals and values to each letter of the word democracy.

D stands for — Division of authority and power
— Dignity and worth of the individual
— Duty-Consciousness
E stands for — Equality
— Ethical values
M stands for — Mutual understanding
— Mass education
O stands for — Objective attitude
— Open mindedness
C stands for — Cooperation
— Classless society
R stands for — Rational approach or thinking
— Respect for others' point of view
— Right relationship between rights and responsibilities
A stands for — 'Appreciation of others' culture, beliefs and point of view
— Adult franchise

C stands for – Cooperative attitude
– Caring and concern for others
– Constructive and creative attitude
Y stands for – Yearning for peace and living together

Chief Characteristics of Democracy in a Broader Sense

From the definitions given above, following characteristics of democracy emerge:

1. Democracy is a way of life. It is an approach to various problems.
2. Democracy as a form of government is based on the consent of the people.
3. Equality, liberty, tolerance, justice and decentralisation are the watch words of democracy.
4. Democracy represents the will of the people. People are sovereign.
5. People elect those representatives who represent their needs and aspirations.
6. These representatives form laws for the people.
7. It is based on the principle of universal adult franchise.
8. Elections are held at regular intervals.
9. There is an election machinery to conduct elections in a fair manner.
10. Citizens enjoy fundamental rights.
11. Citizens have the right to change the government through election.
12. Usually there are several political parties representing various views that participate in elections.
13. All the three organs of the government, i.e., the legislature, the executive and the judiciary are independent and they are supposed to function according to the law of the land.
14. It has faith in the goodness and rationality of man.
15. It recognises the importance of the dignity of man.

16. Every citizen of the prescribed age has the right to contest election.
17. Every citizen possessing the requisite qualifications has the right to contest and hold political post.

DIMENSIONS OF DEMOCRACY

1	2	3	4	5
Economic Dimension	*Educational Dimension*	*Ethical Dimension*	*Political Dimension*	*Social Dimension*
This implies	This denotes	This means faith that an individual is entitled to enjoy full respect for his individuality.	This includes	This incorporates equality of all, irrespective of caste, class, colour, creed, sex and wealth etc.
1. Economic equality as far as possible.	1. Equal opportunities in obtaining education.		1. Participation of the people in government.	
2. Satisfaction of the basic needs of the people.	2. Maximum development of the individual.		2. Election and Adult franchise.	
3. Equality of opportunity in undertaking economic activeties.	3. Sharing of responsibility in running the educationnal system.		3. Division of authority among the Central Government, State Government and Local Bodies.	
4. Freedom from want.	4. Education for all.			

MOST ESSENTIAL ELEMENTS OF DEMOCRACY

1. Equality
2. Liberty
3. Secularism
4. Adult Franchise

Conditions/Requisites for the Successful Working of Democracy

1. Well-knit and well-organised political parties.
2. Social equality.
3. Strong and effective leadership.
4. Universal adult franchise.
5. Economic equality.
6. Literate population.
7. Sound traditions.
8. Decentralisation of power.
9. Spirit of tolerance and mutual goodwill.
10. Rule of the law.
11. No privileges and no discretionary powers at any level.
12. Civic values among the citizens.
13. Belief in non-violence and absence of violence.
14. Eternal vigilance.
15. National, state and regional planning.
16. Periodical elections.
17. Effective election machinery.

RELATIONSHIP BETWEEN DEMOCRACY AND EDUCATION

Democracy and Education

The University Education Commission has explained the relationship of democracy and education in these words, "Democracy affirms that each individual has a unique adventure of life. The function of education is guidance of this adventure for the realisation of the potentialities of each individual."

Prof. Dewey in his book *"Democracy and Education"* has explained very clearly the relationship between education and democracy in these words, "A society which makes provisions for participation in its good of all its members on equal terms and which secures flexible adjustment of its institutions through the interaction of the different forms of associated life is a democratic society. Such a society must have a type of education which gives individuals a personal interest in social changes without introducing disorder."

Prof. K.G. Saiyidain explains the functions of education and democracy in his book *Education, Culture and Social Order* in these words, "Education must be so oriented that it will develop the basic qualities of character which are necessary for the functioning of the democratic life." He lists the following qualities to be developed by education for the democratic life:

(i) Passion for social justice.
(ii) Quickening of social conscience.
(iii) Tolerance for cultural and intellectual differences in others.
(iv) Development of love for work.
(v) Deep and true love for the country.

Significant Implications of Democracy in Education

1. Education is essential to a citizen to function as a voter and a legislator.
2. Education is essential to a citizen to understand and discern intelligently the programmes of political parties.
3. Education is necessary to enable the citizens to prepare themselves for securing the means of livelihood without which a democracy is meaningless.
4. Education is essential to develop such attitudes, skills and knowledge which enable the citizens to participate intelligently in the social and other processes.
5. Education enables an individual to understand the laws of the land and their implications.
6. The right to education becomes a fundamental right in a genuine democracy.
7. The right to vote and the right to participate intelligently in shaping the policies of the State

demands not merely the right to education but the right to education in the language of the people.

8. Education for all is a natural corollary of a democratic set-up.

IMPACT OF DEMOCRACY IN EDUCATION

1	2	3	4	5	6
Democracy and Aims of Education	Democracy and Curriculum	Democracy and Teaching-Learning Process	Democracy and Discipline	Democracy and the Teacher	Democracy and Educational Administration, Organisation and Supervision

I. Democracy and Aims of Education

Following are the aims of education in a democracy.

1. Training students in the art of living together.
2. Development of the capacity to think clearly.
3. Development of the capacity to receive new ideas.
4. Development of the ability to think rationally and scientifically.
5. Development of tolerance.
6. Development of true patriotism.
7. Development of the qualities of leadership.
8. Development of the qualities of followership.
9. Improvement of vocational efficiency.
10. Development of the creative energy of the students.

II. Democracy and Educational Administration. This implies:

1. Principle of sharing responsibility.
2. Principle of equality.
3. Principle of freedom.
4. Principle of cooperation.
5. Principle of justice.

6. Principle of recognising the individual worth.
7. Principle of leadership.

III. Democracy and Curriculum. This means:

1. Education according to 4 A's, i.e., age, ability, aptitude and aim of the students.
2. Emphasis on flexibility.
3. Reconciliation to the needs of the society and the pupils.
4. Provision of core-curriculum.
5. Group activities and group work.

IV. Democracy and the Methods of Teaching

1. Principle of sharing in planning.
2. Use of a variety of methods.
3. Group and project work.

V. Democracy and Discipline

1. Discipline becomes self-discipline.
2. No place for 'flogging'.
3. Student participation in running some of the affairs of the students.
4. Student self-government.

VI. Democracy and the Teacher

1. Teacher as a guide and helper.
2. Teacher as a friend.
3. Creation of a healthy environment.
4. Student-centred teaching-learning process.
5. Very few 'do's' and 'don'ts'.
6. Teacher as a believer in the theory of 'Impression rather than repression'.

VII. Democracy and Mass Education

Education is the birth right of every individual. It implies:

1. Universalisation of elementary education.

2. Adult literacy/education.
3. Continuing education.

FUNCTIONING OF THE SCHOOL ON DEMOCRATIC PRINCIPLES AND PROMOTION OF DEMOCRATIC VALUES IN THE STUDENTS

Following are the important principles and considerations for the realisation of democratic values:

1. *Development of Individuality*: It recognises that the child can develop his individuality only when his native power and capacities are given free play to interact fruitfully with his environment.
2. *Many-sided Development of Personality*: It aims at the many-sided development of the personality of the child.
3. *Individual Differences of Children*: It takes into consideration the individual differences of children.
4. *Provision for Diversified Courses*: It provides for diversified courses.
5. *Respect for the Individuality of the Child*: It respects the individuality of the child.
6. *Freedom of the Child*: The progressive school attaches great value to the freedom of the child.
7. *Rich Environment*: It aims at providing rich and active environment to the child.
8. *Constructive and Creative Activities*: It provides constructive and creative activities. Group work is encouraged.
9. *Social Activities*: It provides activities for social participation.
10. *Development of Curiosity*: It develops lively curiosity and hunger for the acquisition of knowledge.
11. *Manual Work*: It provides opportunities for manual work.

12. *Learning by Experience*: It replaces information by experience.
13. *Atmosphere of Love*. It emphasises atmosphere of love and affection.
14. *No Place for Corporal Punishment*. It gives no place to corporal punishment.
15. *Curriculum in Terms of Activities*. Its curriculum is in terms of different activities and experiences besides school subjects.
16. *Stress on Co-operation*: It stresses co-operative attitude at every stage and in all its activities.
17. *Self-government*: Student self-government on a balanced scale may be introduced under the guidance and supervision of the teachers.
18. *Role of the Teacher*: The teacher plays the role of a friend, philosopher and guide.
19. *Centre of Community Service*: The school serves as centre of community service and is closely linked with community.
20. *International Understanding*: It imparts training in International brotherhood and peace.

6

Empowerment of Women: Role of Education

GENDER BIAS IN GENERAL

Usually gender bias consists of inferior views and prejudices about girls and women. Traditionally people in India seem to have been orthodox in thinking that girls and women are fit for the household jobs only. According to them, a woman's primary duty was to look after the welfare of the family within the confines of her husband's house. For long, they were not considered suitable for administrative and political work. However with the concerted efforts of social reformers, like Raja Rammohan Roy, Swami Dayanand, Swami Vivekananda, Mahatma Gandhi and others, the need to pay more attention to their education and status has been gradually appreciated and several steps in this direction taken. The impact of Western thought has also been quite appreciable.

Here a few illustrations of gender bias are given.

1. Political Institutions in the World

(1) Out of about 200 member countries of the UNO, just about half dozen women occupy the office of the State. In the USA, considered to be one of the most progressive countries there has been no women head of the State. Similar is the case in all European countries, except Germany (2005). Even in Communist countries like the erstwhile USSR (now Russian Federation) and China, no women has occupied the highest office.

Most of the UN Organisations are headed by men.

(2) Women's participation in national parliaments (Fig. 33.1) is very small.

(3) *Right of Vote in Elections to Women.* The USA and Sweden extended adult franchise to women in 1920, France in 1945, Italy in 1948 and Switzerland, popularly known as the home of democracy as late as 1973. India provided this in the first general elections in 1951.

(4) *Literacy Rates.* Only about 80 per cent of women as compared with men are literate in the world.

(5) *Gross Secondary School Enrolment Ratio.* In several regions of the world, secondary school enrolment rates of girls are lower than boys.

GENDER DISPARITY IN INDIA

1. Political Institutions

(i) One women President out of 15.

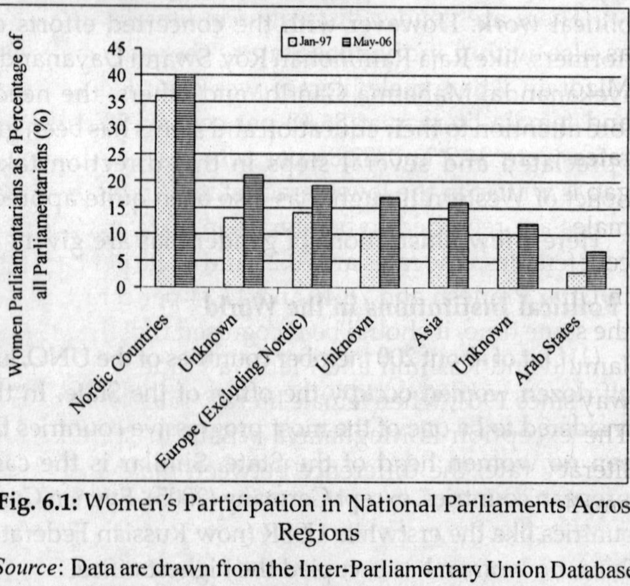

Fig. 6.1: Women's Participation in National Parliaments Across Regions

Source: Data are drawn from the Inter-Parliamentary Union Databases on 'Women in National Parliaments', June 2006.

(ii) One women Prime Minister out of 17.
(iii) No women Vice President out of 12.
(iv) Only about 10% women representation.
(v) Very few Governors.
(vi) Very few Chief Ministers.

2. Administration

1. No women Chief Justice so far.
2. No Head of the Defence Forces.
3. Only about 10 per cent representation in senior administrative services like IAS.

3. Education

1. Not more than dozen Vice-Chancellors out of more than 300 Universities/Deemed Universities etc.
2. No head of NCERT, NIEPA (now NUEPA), CBSE etc.

Gender Disparities in Literacy Rate

There are gender disparities in literacy at all-India level, as also within individual States. The gap was narrowest in Mizoram where male literacy was recorded at 90.69 per cent and female literacy at 86.13 per cent in 2001. In Kerala, the rates were 94.2 and 87.86 per cent respectively in 2001. The gap is widest in the low literacy states. In Bihar, 60.32 per cent males are recorded to be literate in 2001 as against 33.57 per cent females. The rates are 70.23 and 42.98 per cent respectively in Uttar Pradesh and 76.46 and 44.34 per cent in Rajasthan. At the same time, it should be recognised that these States, as also Jammu and Kashmir and Madhya Pradesh, have come a long way since 1961, when female literacy rates were in single digits. The exception is Meghalaya where in spite of low overall literacy rate, the difference between male and female rate is small.

Table 6.1: Gap in Male/Female Literacy Rate (1981-2001)

(in per cent)

Census	*Females*	*Males*	*Literates*	*Male-Female Gap in Literacy Rate*
1981	29.76	56.38	43.57	26.62
1991	39.29	64.13	52.21	24.84
2001	54.16	75.85	65.38	21.69

Note: (i) The literacy rate relate to the population aged seven years and above, (ii) The 1981 Census Literacy rates exclude Assam. The 1991 Census Literacy Rates exclude Jammu and Kashmir.

Table 6.2: Girls Enrolment Per Hundred Boys in 1950-51 and 2004-05

Year	*Primary*	*Upper Primary*	*Secondary*
1950-51	39	18	16
2004-05	88	80	71

Table 6.3: Percentage of Girls to Total Enrolment

Year	*Primary*	*Upper Primary*	*Secondary*	*Higher Education*
1950-51	28.1	16.1	13.3	10.0
2004-05	46.7	44.4	41.5	38.9

Sex Ratio

Sex ratio, measured in terms of the number of women per 1000 men, is representative of women per 1000 men, is representative of gender inequality in India. Biologically, the sex ratio should be in favour of women, and it is so, in almost all countries of the world. However, a pronounced skew in sex ratio in favour of men has been a feature of most states in India. This is largely attributed to lower status of women in Indian society, which contributes to early marriages, lower literacy levels, higher fertility and mortality levels, and affects adverse progress in human development. It is 933 in India.

WOMEN'S WELFARE IN INDEPENDENT INDIA

Constitutional Provisions (Specific Provisions for Women)

Part III - Fundamental Rights

Article 15: Prohibition of discrimination on grounds of religion, race, caste, sex or place of birth.

1. The State shall not discriminate against any citizen on grounds only of religion, race, caste, sex, place of birth or any of them.

2. No citizen shall, on grounds only of religion, race, caste, sex, place of birth or any of them, be subject to any disability, liability, restriction or condition with regard to—

(a) Access to shops, public restaurants, hotels and places of public entertainment; or

(b) The use of wells, tanks, bathing ghats, roads and places of public resort maintained wholly or partly out of state funds or dedicated to the use of the general public.

3. Nothing in this article shall prevent the state from making any special provision for women and children.

Article 16: Equality of opportunity in matters of public employment

(2) No citizen shall, on grounds only of religion, race, caste, sex, descent, place of birth, residence or any of them, be ineligible for, or discriminated against in respect of, any employment or office under the State.

Right against Exploitation

Article 23: Prohibition of traffic in human beings and forced labour

(1) Traffic in human beings and *begar* and other similar forms of forced labour are prohibited and any contravention of this provision shall be an offence punishable in accordance with law.

Part IV – Directive Principles of State Policy

Article 39: Certain principles of policy to be followed by the State

The State shall, in particular, direct its policy towards securing:

(a) That the citizens, men and women equally have the right to an adequate means of livelihood;

(b) That there is equal pay for equal work for both men and women;

(c) That health and strength of workers, men and women, and the tender age children are not abused and that citizens are not forced by economic necessity to enter a vocations unsuited to their age or strength.

Article 42: Provision for just and humane conditions of work and maternity relief

The state shall make provision for securing just and humane conditions for work and maternity relief.

Article 44: Union Civil Code for citizens

The State shall endeavour to secure for all citizens a uniform civil code throughout the territory of India.

Part XV – Elections

Article 325: No person to be ineligible for inclusion in, or to claim to be included in a special, electoral roll on grounds of religion, race, caste or sex.

There shall be one general electoral roll for every territorial constituency for election to either House of Parliament or to the either House of the Legislature of State and no person shall be ineligible for inclusion in any such roll or claim to be included in any special electoral roll for any such constituency on grounds only of religion, race, caste, sex or any of them.

WOMEN'S WELFARE: SOME MILESTONES

I. Milestones towards Women Welfare During British Rule

S. No.	*Year*	*Act/Effort*	*Details*
1.	1815	Women's Education	The Amitya Sabha, founded by Raja Rammohun Roy, emphasised the importance of education of women.
2.	1815	Attack on 'Sati System'	The noted social reformer Raja Rammohun Roy (1774-1833) wrote the first book in Bengali in which he attacked Sati – the practice of burning widows on the funeral pyres of their husbands.
3.	1829	Sati Abolition Act	William Bentinck, the Governor-General of India passed the Sati Abolition Act.
4.	1956	Widow Remarriage Act	Widows were allowed to remarry.
5.	1872	Civil Marriage Act	Some changes were introduced in marriage rules.
6.	1917	Franchise for Women	A delegation of women met the Secretary of India and pleaded for franchise for women.
7.	1927	Women's Conference	All India Women's Conference was set-up.

II. Acts Passed in Independent India

Sl. No.	*Year*	*Act / Effort*	*Details*
1.	1951	Farm Labour Act	Providing break to working women for nursing children.
2.	1952	Employee's State Regulations Act	Providing maternity facilities to women.
3.	1956	Beedi and Cigarette Employees Act	Providing child care system at the place of work.

(*Contd.*)

Sl. No.	*Year*	*Act / Effort*	*Details*
4.	1961	Pre-maternity Care Act	Providing for abortion and maternity leave.
5.	1976	Contract Labour Act	Regulating working hours and maximum 9 hour's work.
6.	1976	Equal Wages Act	Providing for equal wages for man and woman.
7.	1976	Child Marriage Prohibition Act	Providing for abolition of child marriage.
8.	1979	Inter State Migrant Workers Act	Providing for separate public toilet facilities for women.
9.	1986	Women Vulgarity Prohibition Act	Providing for prevention of vulgar exhibition of womanhood.
10.	1961	Dowry Prohibition Act (Amendment Act 1986)	Prohibition of dowry, providing for strengthening enforcement.
11.	1987	Sati Prohibition Act, 1987	Providing for banning Sati practice.
12.	1993	73rd and 74th Constitutional Amendment Act	Providing for 30 per cent reservation for women in Panchayats.
13.	1994	Pre-Natal Diagnostic Technique (Regulation and Prevention of Misuse Act)	Providing for prevention of determination of female foetus in the womb of the mother as illegal.
14.	2004	Equal Rights for Daughters to Ancestral Property.	The Government of India decided on December 15, 2004, to provide by law equal share of ancestral property to daughters along with sons. This is to amend Hindu Succession Act, 1956 which granted unfair benefits to male heirs of a Hindu who died without a will and deprived women the right to seek share in ancestral property.

Department of Women and Child Development

A separate Department for Women and Child Development was set up at the Centre in 1985 to give a distinct identity and provide a nodal point on matters relating to women's development.

National Institute of Public Cooperation and Child Development

The National Institute of Public Cooperation and Child Development (NIPCCD) is an autonomous organisation functioning under the aegis of the Department of Women and Child Development as its technical arm. The objectives of NIPCCD are to develop and promote voluntary action in social development, conduct a comprehensive review of child development and development and promote programmes in pursuance of the National Policy for Children. It also seeks to develop measures for coordination of government and voluntary action in social development and evolve a common framework for organising children's programmes by government and voluntary welfare action.

Central Social Welfare Board

The Central Social Welfare Board (CSWB) was set up in 1953 with the objective of promoting social welfare activities and implementing welfare programmes for women, children and the handicapped through voluntary organisations. The CSWB is unique in the sense that it was the first organisation in post-Independence era to achieve people's participation for implementation of welfare programmes for women and children through non-governmental organisations (NGOs). Presently more than 18,000 NGOs are receiving financial assistance and guidance from the Board. The programmes implemented by the Board include: socio-economic programme for needy/destitute women, condensed courses of education and vocational training courses for women and girls, awareness generation projects for rural and poor women, family counselling centres/voluntary action bureaux, holiday camps for children, welfare extension projects in border areas, and balwadis, crèches and hostels for working women, etc.

EMPOWERMENT OF WOMEN

Meaning of Empowerment of Women

The term 'Empowerment of Women' became popular in India in the 1990s. It implies involving women in decision-making and implementing processes in all areas of national life, including political and administration.

In the 1970s, the term 'welfare' with respect to women was used. In the 1980s, the term 'development' replaced the term 'welfare'. The 1990s replaced the term 'development' with 'empowerment'.

The Tenth Plan aimed at empowering women through the National Policy for Empowerment of Women (2001).

Important Features of the National Policy for Empowerment of Women (2001)

(i) To create an environment through positive economic and social policies for full development of women to enable them to realise their full potential.

(ii) To enable women to enjoy all human rights and fundamental freedoms on equal basis with men in all spheres—civil, cultural, economic, political and social.

(iii) To provide equal access to women to health care, quality education at all levels, career and vocational guidance, employment, equal remuneration, occupational health and safety, social security and public office, etc.

(iv) To strengthen legal systems aimed at elimination of all forms of discrimination against women.

The policy envisages that all Central and State Ministries would drew up time bound Action Plans for women empowerment. They would also consult National/State Commission for Women.

For the realisation of goals, the National Policy lays emphasis on:

1. Strengthening institutional mechanisms.
2. Resource management.
3. Legislation.
4. Gender awareness.
5. Partnership with voluntary Organisation.
6. International cooperation.

Special Initiatives/Achievements for the Empowerment of Women during the Ninth Plan (1997-2002)

- Adoption of Women's Component Plan (WCP) to ensure that benefits from other developmental sectors do not by-pass women and not less than 30 per cent of funds/benefits flow to them from all the women-related sectors. Review of the progress of WCP during the Ninth Plan reveals that funds flowing from one of the women-related Departments (viz. Family Welfare) was as high as 70 per cent of its Gross Budgetary Support of the Ninth Plan; (1997).
- Launching of *Swa-Shakti* to create an enabling environment for empowerment of women through setting up of self-reliant Self-Help Groups (SHGs) and developing linkages with lending institutions to ensure women's access to credit facilities for income-generation activities; (1998)
- *Stree Shakti Puraskars* instituted for the first time in the history of women's development to honour 5 distinguished women annually for their outstanding contribution to the upliftment and empowerment of women; (1999)
- Adoption of a National Policy for Empowerment of Women to eliminate all types of discrimination against

women and to ensure gender justice, besides empowering women both socially and economically; (2001)

- Celebration of the Year 2001 as 'Women's Empowerment Year' for awareness generation to remove negative thinking, besides building up confidence in women through the processes of conscientisation so that they can take their rightful place in the mainstream of the nation's social, political and economic life; (2001)
- Launching of *Swadhar* to extend rehabilitation services for 'Women in Difficult Circumstances'; (2001)

Rashtriya Mahila Kosh

The *Rashtriya Mahila Kosh* (RMK), since its registration in 1993, has established its credentials as the premier micro-credit agency with its focus on women and their economic empowerment through the provision of credit to poor and assetless women in the informal sector. RMK mainly channels its support through Voluntary Organisations, Women's Development Corporation, Women's Cooperative Societies, Block Samitis under the *Swayamsidha* programme.

Economic, Gender Rights and Social Empowerment of Women

Economic Empowerment

Ensuring provision of training, employment and income generation activities with both 'forward' and 'backward' linkages with the ultimate objective of making all women economically independent and self-reliant through:

- Organising women into Self-Help Groups under various poverty alleviation programmes, viz. Swarna Jayanti Gram Swarozgar Yojana (SGSY), Swarna Jayanti Shahari Rozgar Yojana (SJSRY), Rashtriya Mahila Kosh (RMK), Support for Training and Employment Programme (STEP), Training-cum-Production Centres for Women (NORAD), etc. and offering them a range of economic options along with necessary support measures to enhance their capabilities and earning capacities with an ultimate objective of making them economically independent and self-reliant.

- Ensuring that women in the Informal Sector who account for more than 90 per cent are given special attention with regard to improving their working conditions as the same continued to be very precarious without even minimum or equal wages, leave aside other legislative safeguards.
- Ensuring that the employers fulfil their legal obligations towards their women workers in extending child care facilities, maternity benefits, special leave, protection from occupational hazards, allowing formation of women workers, associations/unions, legal protection/ aid, etc.
- Re-training/upgrading the skills of women displaced from traditional sectors due to advancement of technology so that they can take up jobs in the new and expanding areas of employment and formulating appropriate policies and programmes to promote alternative opportunities for wage/self-employment in traditional sectors like khadi and village industries, handicrafts, handlooms, sericulture, small-scale and cottage industries.
- Increasing access to credit for women.

Gender Justice

Eliminating all forms of gender discrimination and, thus, enabling women to enjoy not only *de-jure* but also *de-facto* rights and fundamental freedom at par with men in all spheres, viz. political, economic, social, civil, cultural, etc. through:

- Complete eradication of female foetus and female infanticide through effective enforcement of both the Indian Penal Code, 1860 and the Pre-Natal Diagnostic Technique (Regulation and Prevention of Misuse) Act,

1994 with most stringent measures of punishment so that a very harsh path is set for the illegal practitioners.

- Working out strategies, in close collaboration with the Ministry of Labour, to ensure extension of employment opportunities and thus, remove inequalities in employment—both in work and accessibility.
- Expediting action to legislate reservation of not less than 1/3 seats for women in the Parliament and in the State Legislative Assemblies and thus ensure women in proportion to their numbers reach decision-making bodies so that their voices are heard.
- Arresting the ever-increasing violence against women and the Girl Child including the adolescent girls on top priority with the strength and support of a well-planned Programme of Action.
- Initiating/accelerating the process of societal reorientation towards creating a gender-just society.

Social Empowerment

Creating an enabling environment by adopting various affirmative developmental policies and programmes for development of women.

EDUCATION FOR WOMEN'S EQUALITY AND EMPOWERMENT

The NPE 1986 stipulates that "Education will be used as an agent of basic change in the status of women. In order to neutralise the accumulated distortion of the past, there will be a well-conceived edge in favour of women." For achieving this, "The National Education System will play a positive, interventionist role in the empowerment of women." The NPE's programme includes the following dimensions:

1. Redesigning of courses to develop new values.
2. Redesigning of textbooks to eliminate all sex bias.

3. Training and orientation of teachers for developing sensitiveness to women's issues and their empowerment.
4. Orientation of decision makers and administrators to women issues.
5. Active involvement of educational institutions in enabling women in the process of empowerment of women.
6. According priority to the removal of illiteracy among women through provision of special support services, setting of time-bound targets and effective monitoring.
7. Increasing participation of women in vocational, technical and progressional education at all levels.
8. Following policy of non-discrimination to eliminate stereotyping in vocational and professional courses.
9. Promoting women's participation in non-traditional as well as in existing and emergent technologies.

Mahila Samakhya (MS) Programme

The Programme launched in support of Women's education as envisaged in NPE revolves around the *Sangha* (Village Level Women's Collective) which is considered as the nodal point. The process of mobilising women and creating an environment for women participation in learning is facilitated by a *Sahayogni* (a cluster coordinator in-charge of 10 villages). She is a crucial link between the village *Sangha* and the district implementation unit of the programme. The district implementation unit provides resource support and inputs to meet the needs of women. The district units in turn are supported by a state office.

Mahila Samakkya has expanded its coverage to 40 districts and over 7000 villages.

The *Sangha,* the nodal point of the programme, addresses a wide range of issues relating to the livelihood of women, their education, health, etc. It has taken an active lead in enrolling children, primarily girls, in the village schools.

Achievements Since 1950-51

Table 6.4: Percentage of Girls Enrolment to Total Enrolment by Stages

Year	*Primary (Classes I-V)*	*Upper Primary (Classes VI to VIII)*	*Secondary/ Sr. Secondary/ Intermediate (Classes IX-XII)*	*Higher Secondary (Degree or Above)*
1950-51	28.1	16.1	13.3	10.0
2004-2005	46.7	44.4	41.5	39.4

Table 6.5: Gross Enrolment Ratio (GER) Since 1950-51

	1950-51			*2004-05*		
	Boys	*Girls*	*Total*	*Boys*	*Girls*	*Total*
I. Primary (I-V)	60.6	24.8	42.6	110.7	104.7	107.8
II. Upper Primary (VI to VIII)	20.6	4.6	12.7	74.3	65.1	69.9
III. Elementary (I-VIII)	46.4	17.7	32.1	96.9	89.9	93.5

Table 6.6: Drop-out Rates Since 1960-61

	1960-61			*2004-05*		
	Boys	*Girls*	*Total*	*Boys*	*Girls*	*Total*
I. Primary (I-V)	61.7	70.9	64.9	31.80	15.42	29.00
II. Elementary (I to VIII)	75.0	85.0	78.3	50.49	51.28	50.84
III. Secondary (I-IX)	NA	NA	NA	60.41	63.88	61.92

Observations

- The gap in male-female rate has decreased from 24.84 per cent in 1991 to 21.60 per cent in 2001.
- Female literacy increased by 14.41 per cent, i.e., from 39.29 per cent to 53.7 per cent whereas male literacy increased by 11.17 per cent, i.e., from 64.13 per cent to 75.30 per cent during the last decade.
- Gender equity and women's empowerment is also visible as about 60 per cent of participants and beneficiaries are women.

7

Value Education

VALUE EDUCATION—THE ONLY BASIS OF ESTABLISHING A TRULY DEMOCRATIC, SECULAR AND SOCIALIST SOCIETY

Inculcation of desirable values in the pupils of all ages is absolutely essential for meeting out the crisis of character. In the situation that is rapidly developing, it is equally important for us to give a proper value-orientation to our educational system.

Addressing the one of the most inspiring gatherings ever held at the U.N. in August-September 2000, the U.N. Secretary General called upon the religious and spiritual leaders to 'look within' and to consider what they could do to promote "justice, equality, reconciliation and peace."

There is no doubt that some sort of 'spiritual therapy' is needed for having a value-based society.

MEANING OF 'VALUE'

In the words of Wuchohn, "Value is a conception, emplicit or implicit, distinctive of an individual or characteristics which influence the selection, from available modes and ends of action."

Rokeach defines values, "as an enduring belief, a specific mode of conduct or end along a continuum of relative importance.

John Dewey views a value as, "The value means primarily to prize, to esteem, to appraise, to estimate. It means the act of cherishing something, holding it dear and also the act of passing judgement upon the nature and amounts of values as compared with something else."

W.H. Kilpatrick has explained the concept of values as, "That out of man's capacity for goal seeking behaviour arise his wants and efforts and out of these come in consciously chosen ends (goals) a mean. Because ends conflict, man is led to weigh his goals against each other, when this is done critically enough values emerge."

Henderson in this context observes, "It has been pointed out that man acts to satisfy his wants, anything which satisfies a human want becomes thereby a value. To say that our conduct is motivated by our value is another way of saying that we act to satisfy our wants."

A value stands for ideals men live for. Values are the part and parcel of the philosophy of a nation. They are guiding principles of life which are conducive to one's mental, physical and social health.

CLASSIFICATION OF VALUES

Values have been classified in a number of ways and their meanings also sometimes differ.

1. i. Instrumental Values. ii. Intrinsic or Cultural Values.
2. i. Global Values. ii. Individual Values.
3. i. Essential Values. ii. Personal Values. iii. Social Values. iv. Cultural Values. v. Institutional Values.
4. i. Disciplinary Values. ii. Cultural Values.
5. i. Liberalising Values. ii. Sentimental Values.
6. i. Preparatory Values. ii. Introductory Values. iii. Practical or Utilitarian Values. iv. Conventional Values.
7. i. Traditional Values. ii. Modern Values.

8. i. Material Values. ii. Non-material Values.
9. i. Religious Values. ii. Spiritual Values.
10 i. Secular Values. ii. Scientific Values.
11 i. Individual Values. ii. National Values.
12 i. Ethical Values. ii. Spiritual Values.
13 i. National Values. ii. Global Values.

Instrumental Value: A subject is said to have instrumental value when it is pursued, not for its own sake, but for some ends beyond itself. Instrumental values include preparatory or introductory, practical or utilitarian, socialising and conventional values.

A subject is said to have a *Preparatory* value when it prepares the way for other studies. Arithmetic prepares the way for Algebra. When a particular study introduces us to a number of subjects, it has an *introductory* value. It is identical with the preparatory value. To illustrate we may select Physical Geography which introduces us to a little of Botany, Zoology, Physics and Chemistry. The *practical or utilitarian* value lies in a study of subject whose pursuit is useful inasmuch as it satisfies many wants and needs. The subject is individually and directly practical when the knowledge of the subject is applied directly by the person himself. A person may use his knowledge of hygiene to escape small pox. The same knowledge can, however, be used through other agencies, through society, for example. A subject is said to possess a socialising value when it creates socially desirable habits and reactions, or when it enables us to understand society in its complexities. The socialising value includes moral values too. These moral values refer to certain moral traits that society wants individuals to develop. The *conventional value* implies a value which is conventionally desirable in a subject. Certain subjects may be studied because their knowledge is expected of people of a certain class. Their knowledge is indeed for proper social intercourse and social enjoyment. In the times of Locke, a gentleman was expected to learn Latin, Greek and Grammar because they were necessary in that social set up.

Intrinsic values are inherent in the subjects that we may describe as cultural studies. These have been described by Dewey as the appreciative studies. The resulting experiences in these subjects are worthwhile on their own account. These values that accrue from their studies are in the form of aesthetic pleasures or intellectual joys.

The cultural values have been subdivided into the liberalising and the *sentimental values*. The liberalising value consists in the pleasure that accompanies intellectual insight. The sentimental value, on the other hand, refers to pleasure that emerges when our feelings are exercised. Our feelings may be aroused by the aesthetic, the comic, the social and the moral situation. Drama, Literature, Music, Painting, Sculpture and Religion have, in varying degrees, these values.

Professor Cunningham lays stress on the disciplinary values of the subjects. Their pursuit is important because it gives rise to mental activity and forms sound habits and skills. Each subject, he says, causes certain type of mental operation or discipline. For example, natural sciences produce an attitude of mind characterised by precision which results from observation and reflective thinking. The humanistic sciences produce the discipline of tolerance. Metaphysical sciences, theology and philosophy produce the discipline of unification because in all these the ultimate aim is to achieve harmony and unity in life. The discipline of appreciation is produced by such subjects as painting, music, sculpture and others. The language arts will produce the discipline of expression which consists not only in the training to express oneself but also in being able to understand what others say and write.

Essential Values: These values involve the basic nature of man himself and include elementary physical skills, basic social skills, ability to use symbols such as language and numbers.

Personal Values: These values make a person good for himself.

Social Values: These values are good for the society and form the basis of the relationship of an individual with other people in society.

Institutional Values: These include values established by institutions, political etc.

Global Values: These values pertain to the entire humanity.

ALPHABETICAL CLASSIFICATION OF VALUES

We shall base our discussion regarding traditional and modern values on the basis of the classification of values as compiled by NCERT in its publication entitled *'Documents on Social, Moral and Spiritual Values in Education'* (1979). These values for the sake of convenience are classified here alphabetically.

1. Abstinence
2. Appreciation of cultural values of others
3. Anti-Untouchability
4. Citizenship
5. Consideration for others
6. Concern for others
7. Cooperation
8. Cleanliness
9. Compassion
10. Common cause
11. Common Good
12. Courage
13. Courtesy
14. Curiosity
15. Democratic Decision Making
16. Devotion
17. Dignity of the individual
18. Dignity of Manual Work
19. Duty
20. Discipline
21. Endurance
22. Equality
23. Friendship
24. Faithfulness
25. Fellow-feeling
26. Freedom
27. Forward look
28. Good Manners
29. Gentlemanliness
30. Gratitude
31. Honesty
32. Helpfulness
33. Humanism
34. Hygienic Living
35. Initiative
36. Integrity
37. Justice
38. Kindness
39. Kindness to Animals
40. Loyalty
41. Leadership
42. National Consciousness
43. National Integration
44. National Unity
45. Non-Violence
46. Obedience
47. Patriotism
48. Peace
49. Proper Utilisation of Time
50. Punctuality
51. Purity
52. Quest for Knowledge

53. Regularity
54. Resourcefulness
55. Respect for Others
56. Reference for Old Age
57. Secularism and Respect for All Religions
58. Self-Confidence
59. Self-Control
60. Self-Discipline
61. Self-Duty
62. Self-Help
63. Self-Reliance
64. Self-Respect
65. Self-Restraint
66. Self-Support
67. Sense of Discrimination between Good and Bad
68. Sense of Social Responsibility
69. Simple Living
70. Sincerity
71. Socialism
72. Social Justice
73. Social Service
74. Solidarity of Mankind
75. Spirit of Enquiry
76. Sympathy
77. Team Work
78. Tolerance
79. Truthfulness
80. Universal Love
81. Universal Truth
82. Value for National and Civil Property

TRADITIONAL AND MODERN VALUES

Strictly Speaking, there is no water-tight compartment between the traditional values and modern values. It is also true that there is difference in emphasis on some values with the change of time. However, there are some values like personal purity—self-control, self-discipline, truth, universal love etc. which are of a universal nature.

The following ancient values contained in an ancient Indian invocation are equally relevant even today.

Sarve bhavantu sukhinah

Sarve santu niramayah

Sarve bhadrani pashyantu

Ma kaschit dukha bhag bhavet!

(May all live happily

May all enjoy good health

May all see auspiciousness

May none experience distress
May peace prevail everywhere!)

There is no dividing line between values. However an attempt is made here to distinguish between the traditional values and the modern values in view of the following factors:

1. Modern emphasis on Democratic Values as against traditional Colonial Values.
2. Modern emphasis on Socialist Values as against the traditional emphasis on Capitalist Values.
3. Modern emphasis on Secular Values as against traditional emphasis on Religious Values.
4. Modern emphasis on Scientific Values as against traditional emphasis on Superstitious Values.
5. Modern emphasis on Global Values as against Traditional emphasis on Nationist Values.
6. Modern emphasis on Emotional Integration and National Unity as against the traditional emphasis on Local/Regional Values.

EDUCATION AND NEED FOR INCULCATION OF VALUES

The Kothari Commission has rightly observed, "The expanding knowledge and the growing power (science) which it places at the disposal of modern society must, therefore, be combined with the strengthening and deepening of the sense of responsibility and a keener appreciation of moral and spiritual values."

The National Policy on Education 1986 has very aptly stressed the need for the inclusion of values in the curriculum: "The growing concern over the erosion of essential values and an increasing cynicism has brought to focus the need for readjustments in curriculum in order to make education a forceful tool for the cultivation of social and moral values." The policy has described these values as, "In our culturally plural society, education should foster universal and eternal values, oriented towards the unity and integration of our people. Such value education should help eliminate obscurantism, religious fanaticism, violence, superstition and fatalism." The National Policy further envisaged that "apart from this combative role, value education has a profound positive content, based on our cultural heritage, national goals and universal perceptions. It should lay primary emphasis on this aspect."

VALUE-BASED CURRICULUM IN INDIA

Value-based curriculum is the paramount need of the hour on account of the following facets of life:

- Pluralist nature of our society comprising multi-linguistic, multi-racial and multi-religious groups.
- Existence of a sizeable section of the society below the poverty line.
- Deep-rooted superstitions in people.
- Fatalistic attitude.
- Increased use of 'money power' in democratic elections.
- Widespread prevalence of corruption.
- Consumer culture or materialistic outlook.
- Growth of favouritism.

SCHOOL PROGRAMME FOR DEVELOPING VALUES OF VARIOUS KINDS

Following are the important activities to be undertaken in the school in this regard:

1. Celebration of national festivals.
2. Social service programmes.
3. Emphasis on the unity of all religions, harmony among communities and national integration.
4. Development of scientific temper.
5. Community prayer in the school.

6. Health and cleanliness programmes.
7. Socially useful productive programmes.
8. Citizenship training programmes.
9. Cultural and recreational programmes.
10. Student self-government in schools.
11. Introduction of Information Technology.
12. International understanding.
13. Appropriate teaching-learning situations.

ROLE OF THE TEACHER

The teachers must play an important role in such programmes. The most important aspect is that they should set good examples of conduct and behaviour which the students may imbibe in themselves.

Lastly, it may be stressed that the teachers, the educational workers, the educators, the supervisors, the administrators and above all the parents must try their best to promote value-oriented education.

SYNTHESIS BETWEEN THE TRADITIONAL VALUES AND MODERN VALUES: SYNTHESIS BETWEEN SCIENTIFIC, SECULAR AND SPIRITUAL VALUES

In the attempt to inculcate values through education, we should draw freely upon our own traditions as well as the traditions of other countries and cultures of the world. There are strands within Indian thought itself which can lead to the new outlook appropriate for a modern society, and which can prepare the people for a willing acceptance of life with all its joys and sorrows, its challenges and triumphs. In them, too, we can find inspiration for social service and faith in the future. Mahatma Gandhi, for instance—and some other great leaders of thought—discovered the inspiration for their idealism and their passionate striving for social justice and social reconstruction largely from these sources. It is such re-interpretations and re-evaluations of the past that are now most needed. It is, however, specially important in the world of today that this effort should not be restricted to the national sources only. It would be necessary to draw upon liberalising forces that have arisen in the western nations and which have emphasised among other things, the dignity of the individual, equality and social justice.

India is on the move again with the promise of new renaissance in the making. The most powerful tool in the process of this renaissance and modernisation is education based on secular values on the one hand and on the other on science and technology. In this context we cannot do better than to quote Pt. Jawahar Lal Nehru, "Can we combine the progress of science and technology with the progress of mind and spirit also? We cannot be untrue to science because that represents the basic fact of life today. Still less can we be untrue to those essential principles for which India has stood in the past throughout the ages. Let us then pursue our path to industrial progress with our strength and vigour and at the same time remember that material riches without toleration and compassion and wisdom may well turn to dust and ashes."

The Education Commission 1964-66 has observed, "We believe that India should strive to bring science and the values of the spirit together in harmony and thereby pave their way for the eventual emergence of a society which would cater to the needs of the whole man and not only to a particular fragment of his personality."

Remarks made by Albert Einstein in '*Ideas and Opinions*' in this regard are very enlightening: "It is not enough to teach man a speciality. Through it he may become a useful machine but not a harmoniously developed personality. It is essential that the students require an understanding of and a lively feeling for values. He must require a vivid sense of the beautiful and of the morally good. Otherwise he with his specialised knowledge resembles a well-trained dog rather than a harmoniously developed person."

8

Futurology: Education for the Future Society

MEANING AND ORIGIN OF THE TERM FUTUROLOGY

The term 'futurology' was coined by a German Professor Ossip K. Flechthein in the mid 1940s. He proposed it as a new branch of knowledge dealing with a 'new science of probability'. It implies a detailed critical analysis and reasoning of the states of things which would develop in the future.

The literal meaning of the term futurology is the study of the future.

The discipline of futurology is referred to by the following terms:

(i) Foresight
(ii) Futurism
(iii) Prospective (Latin America)
(iv) *Futuribles* (The name of a Journal also published in France)
(v) Future Studies (Common term used in English-speaking world)

CHIEF CHARACTERISTICS OF FUTUROLOGY

1. It often examines possible as well as probable state of future things from current trends.

2. It attempts to provide a systematic and holistic view based on insights from a wide range of different disciplines.

3. It relies on 'backcasting' i.e., seeking what changes in the

present would be required to arrive at envisioned alternative future state of things on the basis of past and present.

Futurists: Foresight practitioners are called futurists.

Future Studies: This discipline emerged in mid-1960s. It reflects on how today's changes or the lack these of become tomorrow's reality. Among the futurists of the 1960's, important scholars were: Olaf Helmer, Bertrand de Jouvenel, Dennis Gabor, Oliver Markley, Burt Nanus and Wendell Bell.

SUBJECTS AND METHODS OF STUDY OF FUTUROLOGY

The subjects and methods include possible, probable and desirable alternative variations or transformation of the present.

EDUCATION AS A FIELD OF STUDY IN FUTUROLOGY

The USA is a pioneer in taking up education as a field of study in futurology. The studies in the subject began in the 1960s. Since then several countries have developed theories in the area of future education. Several tools have also been developed.

KEY FACTORS IN THE PARADIGM SHIFT IN THE FUTURE EDUCATION

Factor	*Development*
Time	The time factor will no longer be a constraint. Asynchronous education frees the student from the demands of time.
Space	The distance factor will no longer be a constraint. The student can take part in education without being physically present at the teaching institution.
Cost	The pedagogical investment for modern distance education is certainly greater than that of the traditional model, whether in terms of initial outlay or the investment connected with delivering the education. There are two factors, however, which will reduce the overall cost in factors of scale:

(*Contd.*)

Factor	*Development*
	1. The reduction of needs in terms of area and premises; and 2. The appreciable increase in the size of the virtual class.
Relationships	The traditionally vertical teacher-student relationship will evolve towards a more *horizontal* model, in which the teacher becomes a facilitator, expert or colleague and the learner becomes active. In this evolution of roles the group will gain importance as a source for consultation, dialogue and collaboration. Through this mechanism the education is 'received' by the individual in interaction with a group, of which the teachers constitute only one element. Roles are thus completely redefined, and the dynamism of the new roles requires a new student.
Information/ knowledge	The transfer of knowledge is no longer the primary object of education. The student must learn to gather information as the need arises, to evaluate it, and to transform it into knowledge through the relational process.
Market	By easing the constraints of space and time, education will open up to the *global market*, where language will become one of the main constraints on expansion.
Competition/ collaboration	The internationalisation of the education market and the emergence of new entities placed deliberately in the commercial area will intensify competition between educational establishments. In parallel collaboration and strategic alliances on the part of universities will become imperative as the appropriate response to change.
Assessment	The traditional concepts of student assessment based on (examination) results will have to be adapted to new methods in which the assessment of the process will gain more importance so that the measuring of assimilated knowledge can be

(*Contd.*)

Factor	Development
	circumvented and factor more sensitive to the equation of the new *professional* can be integrated: ability to carry out research, to adapt, to communicate, to collaborate, etc.
Type	The distinctions drawn between the various types of education (primary, secondary, technical, university, vocational) will become less important, and the emphasis will be placed on *continuing* education.

(Didier Oilo, *From Traditional to Virtual: The New Information Technologies: Thematic Debate*, UNESCO, 1998)

CHIEF CHARACTERISTICS OF THE FUTURE EDUCATION

1. *Technological Use in Schools*: Schools are likely to go High Tech. They will increasingly make use of laptops, and computers for learning aids. Some of the schools may become virtual institutions.

2. *Domination of Private Schools*: The State school system may see its decline if not demise. An increasing number of parents would prefer privately financed schools. There is likely to be a wide gap in the infrastructure and fee structure of different types of private schools.

3. *Individualised Instruction or Self-Learning*: Internet is likely to be used in general by students to gain knowledge. Schools would offer more opportunities for individualised learning.

4. *Merger of Several Categories of Students: Adult Students with Secondary/High Classes Students*: There may be a merger of some categories of adult students with high school students if technology accelerates enough.

5. *Online Learning*: Teachers will follow online checking method of student's assignments.

6. *Increasing Use of Computers*: As more and more assignments are transferred from paper-borne to an electronic borne media. The students' need for computers will become more pressing.

7. *Chatting*: More students will begin chatting among themselves.

8. *E-mail*: E-mail will become means of storing homework and other information and therefore greater use of computers.

9. *Quality and Quantity of Information*: Quality and quantity of information will increase with a spectacular increase in the use of internet.

10. *Dependence of the Students on the Online Reference Material*: As online reference study guides which cover almost every subject in the school curriculum, will become more and more effective in their coverage of material learned in the classroom, students' dependence on this material will increase.

11. *Freedom to Choose Subjects*: Students would be able to choose any subject at will. They will also be able to decide on what their future career will be and therefore concentrate on its pre-requisites rather than on anything else.

UNESCO AND REFORMS IN EDUCATION

Since its birth, UNESCO has been playing a leading role in stimulating and promoting the reflections and debates on the future of education. Its major reports in this area are:

1. *'Learning to Be' (1972)*: Report published by the International Commission on the Development of Education.
2. International Symposium on the Evolution of the Content of General Education Over the Next Two Decades (1980).
3. *'The Contents of Education: A World View of Their Developments from the Present to the Year 2000 (1987)'* – a publication.
4. International Symposium and Round Table on Education (1989).
5. International Conference on Education (1994).

6. Planning of Higher Education in the Twenty First Century: Role of Management: Report of a Workshop (1995).
7. International Commission on Education for the Twenty-First Century (1993-1996).

The Commission was established at the beginning of 1993. Jacques Delors of France was the Chairman of the Commission. It had 15 members including the Chairman. Dr. Karan Singh, of India's who has been a diplomat and several times Minister *inter-alia* Health and Education, author of several books was one of the members.

The Commission gave its report, in 1996. The report entitled '*Learning the Treasure Within*'.

In the words of the Chairman of the Commission, "The Commission affirms its belief that education has a fundamental role to play in personal and social development."

Four Pillars of Education: According to the Commission, educational structure stands on four pillars:

1. Learning to Know
2. Learning to Do
3. Learning to Live
4. Learning to Be

Accordingly the Commission suggested future reforms in education.

FUTURE SCENARIO OF TENSIONS AND THE ROLE OF EDUCATION

Jacques Delores, Chairman of the International Commission on Education for the Twenty First Century (1993-96) studied the role of future education in the context of the following tensions, although not new, but becoming the central to the problems of the twenty-first century.

The Tension between the Global and the Local: People need gradually to become world citizens without losing their roots and while continuing to play an active part in the life of their nation and their local community.

The Tension between the Universal and the Individual: Culture is steadily being globalised but as yet only partially. We cannot ignore the promises of globalisation nor its risks, not the least of which is the risk of forgetting the unique character of individual human beings; it is for them to choose their own future and achieve their full potential within the carefully tended wealth of their traditions and their own cultures which, unless we are careful, can be endangered by contemporary developments.

The Tension between Tradition and Modernity, which is Part of the Same Problem: How is it possible to adapt to change without turning one's back on the past, how can autonomy be acquired in complementarily with the free development of others and how can scientific progress be assimilated? This is the spirit in which the challenges of the new information technologies must be met.

The Tension between Long-term and Short-term Considerations: This has always existed but today it is sustained by the predominance of the ephemeral and the instantaneous, in a world where an over-abundance of transient information and emotions continually keeps the spotlight on immediate problems. Public opinion cries out for quick answers and ready solutions, whereas many problems call for a patient, concerted, negotiated strategy of reform. This is precisely the case where education policies are concerned.

The Tension between, on the One Hand, the Need for Competition, and on the Other the Concern for Equality of Opportunity: This is a classic issue, which has been facing both economic and social policy-makers and educational policy-makers since the beginning of the century. Solutions have sometimes been proposed but they have never stood the test of time. Today, the Commission ventures to claim that the pressures of competition have caused many of those in position of authority to lose sight of their mission, which is to give each human being the means to take full advantage of every opportunity. This has led us, within the terms of reference of the report, to rethink and update the concept of lifelong education so as to reconcile three forces: competition, which provides incentives; cooperation, which gives strength; and solidarity, which unites.

The Tension between the Extraordinary Expansion of Knowledge and Human Beings' Capacity to Assimilate it: the Commission was unable to resist the temptation to add some new subjects for study, such as self-knowledge, ways to ensure physical and psychological well-being or ways to an improved understanding of the natural environment and to preserving it better. Since there is already increasing pressure on curricula, any clear-sighted reform strategy must involve making choices, providing always that the essential features of a basic education that teaches pupils how to improve their lives through knowledge, through experiment and through the development of their own personal cultures are preserved.

Lastly—Another Perennial Factor—The Tension between the Spiritual and the Material: Often without realising it, the world has a longing, often unexpressed, for an ideal and for values that we shall term 'moral'. It is thus education's noble task to encourage each and every one, acting in accordance with their traditions and convictions and paying full respect to pluralism, to lift their minds and spirits to the plane of the universal and, in some measure, to transcend themselves. It is no exaggeration on the Commission's part to say that the survival of humanity depends thereon.

Education and Points of Emphasis

(1) *Aim of Education*: Education has to face up to this problem now more than ever as a world society struggles painfully to be born: Education is at the heart of both personal and community development; its mission is to enable each of us, without exception, to develop all our talents to the full and to realise our creative potential, including responsibility for our own lives and achievement of our personal aims.

This aim transcends all others. Its achievement, though long and difficult, will be an essential contribution to the search for a more just world, a better world to live in.

(2) *Moral and Cultural Dimensions of Education*: There is, therefore, every reason to place renewed emphasis on the moral and cultural dimensions of education, enabling each person to grasp the individuality of other people and to understand the world's erratic progression towards a certain unity; but this process must begin with self-understanding through an inner voyage whose milestones are knowledge, meditation and the practice of self-criticism.

This message should guide educational thinking, in conjunction with the establishment of wider and more far-reaching forms of international cooperation.

Seen in this context everything falls into place, whether it be the requirements of science and technology, knowledge of self and of the environment, or the development of skills enabling each person to function effectively in a family, as a citizen or as a productive member of society.

(3) *Flexible System of Education*: Education must make its contribution to economic and social development. The education system is all too often blamed for unemployment. This observation is only partly true; above all it should not obscure the other political, economic and social prerequisites for achieving full employment or enabling the economies of underdeveloped countries to take off. As for education, the Commission believes that valid responses to the problems of mismatch between supply and demand on the labour market can come from a more flexible system that allows greater curricular diversity and builds bridges between different types of education, or between working life and further training. Such flexibility would also help to reduce school failure and the tremendous wastage of human potential resulting from it.

Such improvements, desirable and feasible as they are, do not, however, obviate the need for intellectual innovation and the implementation of a model of sustainable development based on the specific characteristics of each county. Given the present and foreseeable advances in science and technology, and the growing importance of knowledge and other intangibles in the production of goods and services, we need to rethink the place of work and its changing status in tomorrow's society. To create tomorrow's society, imagination will have to keep ahead of technological progress in order to avoid further increases in unemployment and social exclusion or inequalities in development.

(4) *Life Long Education and Learning Society*: For all these reasons, it seems to us that the concept of an education pursued throughout life, with all its advantages in terms of flexibility, diversity and availability at different times and in different places, should command wide support. There is a need to rethink and broaden the notion of lifelong education. Not only must it adapt to changes in the nature of work, but it must also constitute a continuous process of forming whole human beings - their knowledge and aptitudes, as well as the critical faculty and the ability to act. It should enable people to develop awareness of themselves and their environment and encourage them to play their social role at work and in the community.

(5) *Increasing the Ability to Learn How to Learn*: Every aspect of life, at both the individual and the social level, offer opportunities for both learning and doing. It is thus very tempting to focus too much on this side of the question, stressing the educational potential of the modern media, the world of work or cultural and leisure pursuits, even to the extent of overlooking a number of fundamental truths: although people need to take every opportunity for learning and self-improvement, they will not be able to make good use of all these potential resources unless they have received a sound basic education. Better still, school should impart both the desire for, and pleasure in, learning the ability to learn how to learn, and intellectual curiosity. One might even imagine a society in which each individual would be in turn both teacher and learner.

SECONDARY EDUCATION/SCHOOL FOR THE FUTURE

Delors Report (1993-1996) or Report of the International Commission on Education for the Twenty-first Century had observed that Secondary education is a "crucial point in the lives of individuals, it is at this stage that young people should be able to decide their own future, in the light of their tastes and aptitudes, and they can acquire the abilities that will make for a successful adult life." The report continued that secondary education "should thus be adapted to take account both of different processes whereby adolescents attain maturity and of economy and social needs."

The Dakar Framework for Action (*UNESCO 2000*) stated, "Education is a fundamental human right. It is the key to sustainable development and peace and stability within and among countries, and thus an indispensable means for effective participation in the societies and economies of the twenty-first century, which are affected by rapid globalisation."

It is in the above context, that UNESCO International Expert Meeting on "General Secondary Education in the Twenty-first century: Trends, Challenges and Priorities" was held in Beijing, People's Republic of China, from 21 to 25 May 2001.

The meeting focused on the following three dilemmas of secondary education:

- In respect of mass and selective schooling.
- In respect of general and selective (vocational) education.
- In respect of cognitive and behavioural outcomes.

These recommendations are valid for India also.

Main Recommendations

Mass and Selective Schooling

- Countries should continue to be committed to the goal of mass Secondary Education as a minimum in terms of policy and provision.

- Commitment to universal access to Secondary Education as an aspiration should be maintained with efforts to remove barriers and obstacles as well as build on strengths and opportunities especially for girls.
- Serious attention be given to making adequate provision for those not selected into Secondary Education, those who drop out or leave before completing the cycle and those denied access to their preferred streams.
- Where there is not full transition from Primary to Secondary and/or from lower Secondary to upper Secondary, efforts must be made to accommodate all those who are eligible through alternative provisions. Where this is not possible, available places should be allocated equitably and transparently.
- Mass access to Secondary Education will require partnership between governments and other providers (private, NGOs, etc.), but governments should seek to safeguard the interests of learners by ensuring that quality standards are maintained by all providers.
- The structure of programmes and streaming practices should be reviewed to offer greater flexibility and choice to learners in the selection process, including the option to return to a preferred stream.
- Future orientation at Secondary Education should be towards greater quality and diversity of what is provided, more flexibility in the organisation of learning and greater responsiveness to the needs and circumstances of learners.

General and Selective (Vocational) Education

- The Secondary Education system should focus on links between academic and vocational subjects and their interdependence in the overall education of adolescent learners of both genders.
- Secondary Education is about preparation for life and should reflect the reality of life in the twenty-first

century that encompasses a seamless to-and-fro between continued learning and the world of work.

- The nature of vocational subjects, the way in which they are organised and taught, as well as the recognition given to them determine their status in the Secondary school curriculum.
- Secondary Education including Vocational Education needs to address not only the human resource needs of the society but also the development needs and aspirations of the individual.
- There is a strong trend in Secondary Education in most countries to include some element of Vocational Education for all learners. Some countries are experimenting with ways of providing such joint education to different population groups, including migrants, isolated rural populations and learners in regular secondary schools.
- Incorporating Vocational Education into Secondary Education can be expensive resulting in poor quality teaching and a lowering of status of these subjects. Innovative and cost-effective strategies to overcome this problem have included contracting out the teaching of subjects to nearby specialist schools and centres or creating different ways of teaching Vocational disciplines that are less demanding in terms of equipment, materials and practically trained instructors.
- As the trend of life-long learning is becoming clear, Secondary Education is adjusting to this reality by developing flexible structures and varied options in their programmes, as well as having stronger links to the world of work.

Cognitive and Behavioural Outcomes

- There is recognition that academically based education does not adequately address students' needs in terms of realising their full potential, especially in a context of rapid economic, cultural and social change and gender based discrimination.

- Given the declining role of other socialising agencies. Schools should take greater responsibility for helping learners acquire life-skills.
- The emerging role of teachers (notably as facilitators), their status, integrity and commitment are essential for implementing life-skills education successfully. The quality of pre-service and in-service teacher training is critical in this regard.
- Teaching methods, school facilities and services should be developed and adapted to provide life-skills/ behavioural education.
- The role of Secondary school principals needs to be consistent with this new reality.
- Education decision-makers need to be sensitised to the consequences of their choices based on evidence of such factors as the links between academic success and personal and community well-being.
- A multi-sectoral approach involving government ministries, NGOs local communities, etc. is essential for successful implementation of this kind of education.

9

Future Education in India

The National Council of Educational Research and Training, New Delhi, usually called the academic wing of the Ministry of Human Resource Development, Department of Education, Government of India, published in 1986 a book entitled *School Education in India: Present Status and Future Needs,* which contained the views of the eminent educators of the country.

POINTERS TOWARDS FUTURE REFORMS IN EDUCATION: SUGGESTIVE MODELS

Notwithstanding the time gap, these views are still relevant and provide useful pointers. Here, three models are briefly reviewed.

I. PROF. MALCOLM S. ADISESHIAH'S MODEL

Prof. Malcolm S. Adiseshiah, a great scholar and educationist in an article *'Educational Perspectives'* described the position in the beginning of the 21st century as "Education of the future will be life-long—a glimpse of a great and revolutionary truth will emerge that education is not a spatial monopoly of something called the school and college; that it is not a time-bound learning experience; that there is no such thing as childhood education, adolescent education, youth education, or adult education. There is just education which is a way of life, a life-long way of life. Every year, every month, everyday, from the cradle to the grave, a person will be learning, open to learning and given the opportunity to learn in the home, school, university, factory, farm, hospital, office, cooperative, temple, trade union, political party, cinema and club. Education will be open. Schools without walls, polyvalent classes, integrated schools, universities of the air, will be juxtaposed with firms, farms, factories and business houses as education extension agents with their survey documentation and research facilities. The whole wide-open area of self-instruction, similar to what is taking place in our rural areas, will be operative. Let us not forget that for the farmer and his wife the farm is the school, what they do in their daily life is their curriculum of learning. Their experience in dealing with their daily survival problem is the substance of their evaluation. Life-long education will be a fact of life".

Prof. Adiseshiah suggested the following educational model for meeting the future needs:

1. *Non-formal Education System*: Launching the non-formal education sub-system for the two priority groups—school drop-outs in the age group 6-14 and working adult illiterates in the age group 15-40, evolving, devising functional curricula, producing learning materials, mobilising teaching resources from trained teachers as well as progressive farmers, engineers, musicians, dramatists and sportsmen and using existing buildings, labs and workshops for running the concentrated courses.

2. *Multiple Entry Points*: Reorganising the existing formal education sub-system into multiple entry and exit points at its different levels so that students could enter, leave and re-enter the school and university system at anyone of several points to answer the call of work in the home, farm, factory or office, continue their education through organised non-formal programmes.

3. *Establishing Relationships*: Establishing the relationship between the two sub-systems involving the nexus between their educational content, methods and technologies of teaching and learning.

4. *Vocationalisation of Secondary Education*: Vocationalising the second level of education.

5. *Important Components of Education*: Things like computerised instruction, open learning systems undifferentiated curricula for rural-urban and male-female populations, inter-disciplinary approaches to teaching, integration of education and work and establishment of a value system which would promote international understanding, peace and harmony will become some of the important components of education in the beginning of the 21st century.

II. PROF. S.V.C. AIYA'S MODEL

S.V.C. Aiya, a former Director of NCERT in an article 'School Science Curriculum Dynamics' incorporated in the same book visualised the scenario for 2000 A.D. as, "Inadequate control of population will create serious problems on the food and health fronts, requiring a specific orientation of school science towards agriculture and preventive medicine.

"Even in agriculture, the demand for unskilled and illiterate labour will decrease. Skilled workers must be mentally prepared to learn, even on their own, new jobs and move to them. Apart from similar qualities, technicians must have proficiency in an international language like English and must be capable of innovating to fill gaps between old and new techniques, etc. Technologists including management personnel, must be familiar with the use of computers, statistical methods, etc. It is their responsibility to reduce pollution, prevent upsetting of the ecological balance and more generally, everything that harms society. They have to instil in society a sense of duty and of social purpose. They have to persuade those concerned to move to new technologies and guard against obsolescence.

"Capacity for logical, orderly and exact expression, ability to properly comprehend technical literature, often in a language other than their mother tongue, and proper realisation of social responsibilities appear to be pre-requisites for skilled workers, and to a much greater extent for technicians and technologists. These qualities have to grow from education at the school level. Hence the humanities and social sciences will go together with science. So far as science is concerned, the forecast indicates that much greater attention has to be paid to application. In addition there is need to move children at school even directly into technology."

III. FUTURE SCENARIO AND KIRPAL'S MODEL OF FUTURE EDUCATION

Dr. P.N. Kirpal, a former Secretary, Ministry of Education, Government of India (now known as Ministry of Human Resource Development, Government of India) in an article published in a book *'School Education in India: Present Status and Future Needs'*, NCERT, 1986, visualised the future scenario in terms of 12 problems. He referred to the three great explosions of accelerated development, three crucial issues contending for mastery, three deep conflicts requiring peaceful resolution and balanced synthesis and three poignant gaps portending grave dangers and fateful challenges. Dr. Kirpal further observed, "Some of these twelve problems have plagued several civilisations of the past, but in the 21st century they can threaten the entire humanity and consequently call for global efforts to overcome the evil and nurture the good implicit in the choices and solutions that may be offered and taken."

Three Explosions:

(1) Explosion of Population;
(2) Explosion of Knowledge, and
(3) Explosion of Expectations.

Three Issues:

(1) Issues of War and Peace;
(2) Issues of Man and Environment; and

(3) Issues of Culture and Technology

Three Conflicts:

(1) Conflict between the Inner Man and the Outer Man;
(2) Conflict between Freedom and Social Organisation; and
(3) Conflict between Tradition and Modernity.

Three Gaps:

(1) Gap between Developed and Developing Countries;
(2) Gap between Knowledge and Wisdom; and
(3) Gap between Power and Love.

Ten Principles for the Transformation of Education for Future Needs

Dr. Kirpal suggests ten principles for a profound renewal and transformation of education:

1. Our thinking should be hard and without rhetoric.
2. Education is synonymous with life.
3. Education is a comprehensive national task involving all people and all society.
4. Integrated education should serve man and social development.
5. Value-oriented education is essential for balanced personality and harmonious society.
6. Indian education should draw upon the growing corpus of international education and enrich it by its own contributions.
7. Education should support and strengthen a great cultural renaissance.
8. Education should help development by cooperative enterprise.
9. The defences of peace are best built in the minds of men.
10. The use of new technology calls for great care and discrimination to absorb it into the national ethos and safeguard moral and cultural values.

FUTURE SCHOOLS AND CLASSROOMS OF INDIA

Following are the characteristics of new schools:

I. Philosophy or Objectives of Future Schools

The Delors Commission Report or the Report of the International Commission on Education (1993-1996) has outlined the philosophy of education on four pillars and the schools must base their programmes accordingly.

1. Learning to Know
2. Learning to Do
3. Learning to Live Together
4. Learning to Be.

1. *Learning to Know*. Learning to know implies:

(i) Concentrating on a small number of concepts.
(ii) Combining a sufficiently broad general knowledge with the opportunity to work in depth on a small number of objects.
(iii) Learning to learn so as to benefit from the opportunity education provides throughout life.

2. *Learning to Do*: Learning to do means:

(i) Acquiring not only occupational skill but also move broadly the competence to deal with many situations and work in teams.
(ii) Learning to do in the context of students' various social and work experiences which may be informal.

3. *Learning to Live Together*. This means:

(i) Developing an understanding of other people.
(ii) Appreciating the spirit of interdependence.

(iii) Managing conflicts in a spirit of respect for the values of pluralism, mutual understanding and peace.

4. *Learning to Be*: It implies:

(i) Bettering development of one's personality.
(ii) Enabling the student to act with greater autonomy.
(iii) Developing power of judgment.
(iv) Developing personal responsibility.
(v) Paying due regard to all aspects of person's potential, i.e., memory, reasoning, aesthetic sense, physical capacities and communication skills.

II. Structuring of the School

Schools, as social institutions, may need to rethink the way they are structured. At present they tend to be based on a nineteenth century hierarchical scientific management model: the superintendent is the manager, the teacher is the worker and the student is the product. Other organisational models for schools may need to be considered if students' development as whole persons is to be enhanced. Rather than considering how to prepare young people for the future, we need to think about preparing for the future with the help of young people through their active participation in and involvement with constructive and cooperative educational environments.

III. Classrooms as Mini Social Realities

In the classroom a "pedagogy of democratic fellowship" can be created in which children collaborate and support each other in their learning. Such classrooms can be mini social realities in which students assume different roles including those of leadership. Teachers are facilitators, organisers and managers of the learning—in this way, they focus not so much on what they are to teach but on supporting their students' learning. In this way, values are imparted through action and interpersonal behaviour in the classroom.

IV. Teaching of Science

A number of issues for the teaching and learning of science will need consideration:

(1) *Science Based on Daily Life Activities*: All students at school should have exposure to science education. However, school science is often divorced from people's everyday understandings. As a result, what is learnt in school is forgotten once examinations have been taken—the learning does not carry over to people's daily lives. If the contexts chosen for science work can draw more on people's daily life experience and their own ideas, then it is more likely that this gap can be bridged. Teaching the science involved in the working of everyday devices, such as farm tools may be helpful in this respect as well as not requiring expensive laboratory provision. However, low-cost science equipment will still be required to meet the needs of developing countries.

(2) *Science as an Enquiry*: In school science courses more emphasis will need to be placed on science as enquiry, as an exciting way of finding out about the world, rather than as a body of knowledge. We need to teach less but teach it more effectively. The local environment should become the laboratory of education, not only in the study of science, but in other areas, such as history and the social sciences.

(3) *Humanistic View of Science*: Science courses should give students the opportunity to consider the social, economic and ecological impact of scientific and technological innovations. The flavour of science as a human pursuit can be given through student's own enquiries. By developing testing and comparing ideas within a group, students can realise that others may have different ideas of their own and can appreciate the way science itself proceeds. Studies of the way scientific ideas have changed over the times, how different societies have developed different theories, and how scientific controversies have occurred in scientific knowledge.

(4) *Environmental Science*: Environmental science will have an important place in helping young people appreciate the

interdependence of living things and the fragile balance in the biosphere. For this locally based case studies would be appropriate and are most likely to stimulate the interest of students.

V. Equality of Opportunity

Equality of opportunity is central to our concerns. It is well-known that in most countries present curricula and teaching methods result in girls achieving less well on physical science courses than boys. The orientation towards the science taught, the way it is presented and the methods of teaching will need to be reviewed to address this problem. The teaching of science to girls as well as boys should be seen in the context of career guidance and counselling in order that equality of opportunity between men and women can be realised in education and training.

VI. Refraining our View of Technology

Our view of technology may also require reframing. There is a tendency for technologies to be viewed as ways of exploiting and controlling the environment to specific ends. In the future, technologies will continue to be developed which meet basic human needs in ways which are appropriate to each culture. Now, with our recognition of factors, such as, the limited physical resource of the earth and the delicate balance that needs to be maintained in the biosphere, we can no longer afford to neglect the various side effects that a technological innovation may have. There will always be costs as well as benefits to be considered as a result of any new technological innovation. Additionally, the role of technology in helping to solve environmental problems needs to be studied.

In a sustainable world there will be need for technological developments and enterprise, not only of a high technology nature, but low cost intermediate technologies will be required. Technology teaching tends to be undervalued compared with science teaching. We suggest that, if we are to develop enterprising students, there may be a case for technology to have a more prominent place in the curriculum.

Technology courses are being implemented in schools in a number of countries. These give students the opportunity to design, construct and evaluate devices or systems which can be chosen to address needs in the students' own environment. In developing and evaluating products in this way, students can also be given the opportunity to consider the costs and benefits of the innovation and hence see the activity in social and environmental terms.

VII. Languages and Language Teaching

A policy for the teaching of languages is needed both to enable people with different mother tongues within a country to communicate and participate in that society and to provide for foreign language teaching to be a high priority in the progressively interconnected world of the twenty-first century. With mass communication now operating on a global scale, there is a real possibility of the English language becoming progressively dominant. However, the importance of preserving the rich cultural heritages embodied in the world's variety of languages was recognised as being essential.

In considering language education for the twenty-first century, the following points were made:

(a) Mother tongue, or the language of the home should be used in the beginning years of schooling where possible. Reading and writing skills in the mother tongue can later be built on in the context of lifelong education.

(b) Foreign languages in schools will require greater attention.

VIII. Communication of Better Quality

Increased communication is needed between teacher, other professional personnel in the school and peer groups. Social learning, human relationship skills values, attitudes, etc. can be stimulated and facilitated in peer groups, provided that teachers and other professionals can offer support and supervision.

IX. Social Sciences in the Curriculum

At a more fundamental level, it is a question of helping pupils to acquire, as they embark on life, the ability to interpret those things that mainly affect their personal future and the future of society as a whole. From this point of view support from the social and human sciences is essential, insofar as they relate both to life itself and to social phenomena. Needless to say, history and philosophy should also occupy an important place in such multidisciplinary research: philosophy because of its role in forming that critical outlook which is indispensable to the functioning of democracy and history because of its irreplaceable role in broadening the individuals horizons and raising awareness of collective identities. The teaching of history should, however, transcend the national context and should encompass a social and cultural dimension, in order that knowledge about the past may lead to a better understanding and a truer appreciation of the present. There is new strategy to be worked both by those who decide the main lines of emphasis of education policy and by those who draw up curricula. The aim would be to integrate the achievements of the social sciences into a global approach whereby a broad understanding of past and present could be attained.

X. Democratic Functioning of the School

With the emerging new democracies, an increasing number of countries are adopting democratic principles of political organisation. This involves a wide range of actors in the decision-making process, including various experts and diverse members of civil society. The challenges occasioned by this new political context go far beyond the establishment of formal democratic mechanisms to include the transformation of the daily life of the citizenry itself. This results in a greater emphasis on shared responsibility in decision-making. This movement involves an increasing emphasis on critical thinking, freedom of expression, the free flow of information and on a philosophy of human rights, with particular to the rights of the individual.

Education in tolerance and respect for other people, a prerequisite for democracy, should be regarded as a general and ongoing enterprise. Values in general and tolerance in particular cannot be taught in the strict sense: the desire to impose from the outside predetermined values comes down in the end to negating them, since values only have meaning when they are freely chosen by the individual. At the very most, therefore, schools may facilitate the daily practice of tolerance by helping pupils to allow for the point of view of others and by encouraging the discussion of moral dilemmas or cases involving ethical choices, for example.

(This aspect of democracy has been taken up in an earlier chapter).

XI. Teaching of Life Skills

Given the declining role of other socialising agencies schools should take greater responsibility for helping learners acquire life-skills. The emerging role of teachers (notably as facilitators), their status, integrity and commitment are essential for implementing life-skills education successfully. The quality of pre-service and in-service teacher training is critical in this regard.

XII. Teaching Methods

Teaching methods, school facilities and services should be developed and adapted to provide life-skills/behavioural education.

XIII. New Role of the Heads of Schools

The role of heads of school needs to be consistent with this new reality. Education decision-makers need to be sensitised to the consequences of their choices based on evidence of such factors as the links between academic success and personal and community well-being. A multi-sectoral approach involving government ministries, NGOs local communities, etc. is essential for successful implementation of this kind of education.

XIV. Broad Based Work Places

Education for the workplace of the future will need to be broadly based during the early years. One way of creating a flexible workforce for the twenty-first century will be to continue the broad general education currently characteristic of primary school education in most countries. This should be continued and general education should extend at least into the early years of secondary education. Primary school students need to be introduced to the concepts related to the world of work at an early age so that they can understand the role of work in our socio-economic system. The point of time when vocational education should be introduced into the educational system will depend greatly on the stage of development and the economic structure of the country or region involved.

XV. Use of New Technology

ICT (Information and Communication Technology will be used widely in educational institutions.

XVI. Teachers for Future Education in India: Radical Change in the Role

The role of the teachers of the future would go a radical change in the future. They would in the real sense would play the role of facilitators of information and knowledge. They would guide the students as 'how to learn'. Emphasis will be on guiding the students. They would be well-versed in the use of ICT in education. A variety of teaching-learning methods would be used.

XVII. Parental Education

Support by society for the careers of children and counselling during their early years. This may include parent education and enabling parents or those with the primary care for young children to have adequate time to spend building sound relationships with them. In societies where parents, due to work obligations, have less time at home, schools are being expected to shoulder the responsibility for children's moral development. However, development of this kind occurs through experience within an environment and formal teaching cannot succeed by itself. There will need to be a partnership with other agencies in society including politicians and the media to address this issue.

XVIII. Non-Military National Service

Some developing countries have introduced a concept of non-military national service. This encourages young people to provide services to their communities and nations at several stages during and after their formal education. This process is also a very effective introduction to the world of work, the development of work ethics and encourages the commitment to public service.

XVIX. Other Programmes

Other programmes include:

(i) Provision of inclusive education.
(ii) Provision of compensatory education.
(iii) Elimination of gender bias.
(iv) Strengthening equity.

10

Agencies of Education: School as an Agency of Education

MEANING AND SIGNIFICANCE OF AGENCIES OF EDUCATION

It is rightly observed by Counts that "The school is but one among many educational agencies." The common belief that education is confined to schools and colleges is not entirely true. No doubt schools and colleges do occupy the most predominant place in the society as educational institutions. But when we use the word 'education' to denote the idea of the all-round development of the personality of the individual, we must recognise the role of other agencies of the society besides the schools and the colleges. Schools function for a short time daily. They function for nearly seven months only during the year. The rest of the time of the students is spent outside the school premises—in the family, in the neighbourhood and with the peer groups. They are influenced by mass communication, media and other agencies like social education centres, libraries etc.

According to some educators, of all the education we receive, we learn one-fourth from our teachers, one-fourth from books, one-fourth from our colleagues and one-fourth from the overall environment. This indicates the type of education and the multitude of agencies of education.

Education in a wider sense takes place from the womb to the tomb, i.e., from the conception to cremation. Education is a life-long process. Education goes on whether we are aware of it or unaware of it. Thus there are several types of social institutions that impart education. There are active as well as passive agencies of education. Likewise there are formal, non-formal and informal agencies of education. They are agencies of education run and managed by the Government. Private agencies are also involved in running different types of educational institutions.

Education imparted in formal agencies is called formal education. Education given in non-formal agencies is called non-formal education. Education received in informal ways is called informal education.

While discussing different types of agencies, it may be borne in mind that teachers are not the only educators. As observed by T. Ramount, "Let us agree to recognise explicitly that in a real sense teachers are not the only educators. In other words it is life that educates, the school provides a part of life's experience."

The agencies of education, we mean various sources, i.e., the institutions and organisations that play their role in varying degrees in the process of education.

BROAD CLASSIFICATION OF AGENCIES OF EDUCATION – I

	1. Formal Agencies of Education		*2. Informal Agencies of Education*		*3. Non-formal Agencies of Education*
1.	School	1.	Art Gallery	1.	Adult and Social Education Centres
2.	College	2.	Cinema	2.	Play ground (when regular physical education is organised)

(*Contd.*)

	1. Formal agencies of Education		*2. Informal Agencies of Education*		*3. Non-formal Agencies of Education*
3.	Home or Family (in the Past)	3.	Home/Family	3.	Radio (Educational Programmes)
4.	Church (in the past)	4.	Library	4.	T.V. (Educational Programmes)
5.	Adult school (on regular basis)	5.	Museum	5.	Professional Organisations like Teachers' Associations when they organise seminars, workshops etc.
6.	Open school (when contact classes are also arranged)	6.	Peer group	6.	Clubs when educational talks etc. are organised.
7.	T.V. (When used as an integral part of the curriculum and pre-telecast and post-telecast lessons are organised)	7.	Play ground (when not supervised by the teacher)	7.	Cinema (When educational pictures are organised)
8.	Radio (When used as an integral part of the curriculum and pre-broadcast and post-broadcast lessons are organised)	8.	Press	8.	Internet (When some educational course is organised)

(Contd.)

	1. Formal agencies of Education		*2. Informal Agencies of Education*		*3. Non-formal Agencies of Education*
9.	State	9.	Reading Room	9.	Correspondence Institutions
		10.	Radio (Normal Programme)	10.	Open Learning Institutions
		11.	Television (Normal)	11.	Distance Learning Institutions
		12.	Voluntary Organisations like Bharat Sewak Samaj, Boy Scouts etc.		
		13.	Internet		

AGENCIES OF EDUCATION: CLASSIFICATION NO. II

Active Agencies of Education	*Passive Agencies of Education*
1. The Family	1. Cinema
2. The School	2. Radio
3. The Community	3. T.V.
4. The Religion	4. Internet
5. The State	5. Library
6. Social Clubs	6. Magazines
7. Peers	7. Newspapers
8. Neighbourhood	8. Market places
	9. Reading Room

AGENCIES OF EDUCATION: CLASSIFICATION NO. III

Formal	*Informal*	*Commercial*	*Non-Commercial*
(1)	(2)	(3)	(4)
1. School	1. The Family	1. Cinema	1. Dramatic Clubs
2. Religious Institution	2. General Games	2. Radio	2. Social Welfare Centres
3. Library	3. The State	3. T.V.	3. Sports Club
4. Art Galleries	4. The Peer Group	4. Clubs	4. Scouting and Guiding
5. Museum	5. The Community	5. Newspaper	5. Youth Welfare Clubs
6. Zoo	6. The Society	6. The Press	6. Adult Education Centres
7. Organised Games			

AGENCIES OF EDUCATION: CLASSIFICATION NO. IV

(1)	(2)	(3)	(4)
Government Run	Government Aided	Government Unaided	Semi Government

Note: There are several ways of classification

Formal Agencies of Education and Formal Education

Formal agencies of education like schools and colleges impart formal education. These agencies are consciously and deliberately planned to bring about specific influences on the educand. They have regular working hours. They prepare students for taking public examinations on regular basis. Usually they employ full time staff. They follow prescribed curriculum and textbooks. They have to conform to rigid departmental rules and regulations.

Informal Agencies of Education and Informal Education

The informal agencies do not follow any set pattern of instruction or education. In fact they impart education incidentally. Education is not organised deliberately in these institutions. These are informal groups. Education is indirect. One may learn without being conscious of it. Nevertheless influence of informal agencies of education is quite significant.

Non-Formal Agencies of Education

'Flexibility' is the key-word in the case of non-formal agencies of education. The system is an 'open one' with regard to: (1) Admission (2) Curricular work, (3) Place of instruction, (4) Mode of instruction, (5) Time and duration of instruction (6) Regular/temporary/part time staff. Open School, Open University, Open Learning Institutions and agencies imparting correspondence education come under non-formal agencies of education. Adult education agencies are usually placed under this category.

NO WATERTIGHT DIVISION OF AGENCIES OF EDUCATION

There is no clear-cut dividing line in classifying educational agencies into formal, non-formal and informal agencies. Even a school can take the form of a non-formal agency of education when it organises adult education classes and programmes. Students in the school acquire a good deal of education through informal contacts with the peers and the teachers. The press, the radio and the T.V. are normally termed as informal agencies of education. However, when they take up occasional programmes of formal education, they assume the form of non-formal agencies of education. Regular school broadcasts and T.V. lessons based on the school curriculum may be considered as programmes of formal education and radio and T.V. as agencies of formal education.

The entire programme of correspondence/distance education/open education may be classified both formal as well as non-formal, depending upon the type and mode of educational activity.

An adult school which follows a regular programme of education comes under the category of formal agency of education. However, when it is used for educational work, for sometime only it is placed under the category of non- formal agency of education. Recreational programme of an adult school may be placed under the category of informal education and this comes under the category of an informal agency of education.

With the increasing use of new educational technology and science and especially information communication technology (ICT), it has become very difficult to divide educational agencies into water tight compartments.

BROAD COMPARISON BETWEEN FORMAL AND NON-FORMAL EDUCATION

		Formal Education Agency	*Non-Formal Education Agency*
1.	Learners	It caters to lear-ners who are in a position to attend full time	It caters to learners who cannot go to school or have dropped. It also includes learners who want to improve their quailfi-cations by studying at home
2.	Aims	To get a certificate or degree needed for a job or self-employment	(i) To increase knowledge and skills
			(ii) To better qualifications
			(iii) To pursue studies for self-satisfaction
3.	Place	An educational institution—school or college—full time	No specific place—can be home, factory, farm, library, open space etc.
4.	Age	Usually prescri-bed ages	Any age

(*Contd.*)

		Formal Education Agency	Non-Formal Education Agency
5.	Grade	Students are grouped into classes	Usually no grouping
6.	Curriculum	Rigid and fixed	Curriculum not fixed
7.	Textbooks	Prescribed textbooks	Usually no prescribed textbooks
8.	Examination	Examination at regular intervals. Written tests. Essay and short answer	Normally no examination Assign-ments
9.	Teachers	Teachers usually on full time basis	Usually part time teachers
10.	Methods of Teaching	Direct teaching methods. Face to face teaching. Lecturing	Contact programmes, radio, T.V. Correspondence lesson, very little face to face teaching
11.	Status	Usually high status	Usually not considered at par with formal agency of education

SCHOOL AS AN AGENCY OF EDUCATION

IMPORTANCE OF SCHOOL AS A SOCIAL INSTITUTION AND A FORMAL AGENCY OF EDUCATION: SELECT VIEWS

A school is one of the most important formal agencies of education. It plays a very significant role in discovering, and moulding the innate capacities, attitudes, habits and ideas of the children with a view to producing well-balanced personalities: aesthetically rich, culturally refined, emotionally stable, mentally alert, morally sound, physically strong, socially efficient and spiritually enlightened.

Following quotations of the eminent thinkers illustrate suitably the importance of the school:

1. In the words of *Kandel*, "The school exists to accelerate

the impact of the essential aspects of culture which prevails in the society".

2. *J.S. Ross* observes, "Schools ought to stress the duties and responsibilities of individual citizen. They ought to train their pupils on the spirit of cheerful willing and effective service".

3. *H.G. Wells* has remarked, "A world whose schools are unreformed is an unreformed world".

4. According to *Dewey*, "The school is primarily a social institution—an effective agency in bringing the child to share in the inherited resources of the race, and to use his own powers for social ends".

5. According to *K.G. Saiyidain*, the school is a centre of vigorous life. It is in direct intimate contact with the realities of the life around, reflecting the best and worthiest of its features which are simple enough to appeal to the child.

6. *The Secondary Education Commission* (*1952-53*) outlines the functions of the school as, "The secondary school must make itself responsible for equipping its students adequately with civic as well as vocational efficiency—and the qualities of character that go with it—so that they may be able to play their part worthily and competently in the improvement of national life. They should no longer emerge as helpless, shiftless individuals who do not know what to do themselves".

7. *The Education Commission* (*1964-66*) observed, "The destiny of India is now being shaped in her classroom". This clearly explains the significant role of the school in social change.

8. *P.C. Nunn* describes the role of the school in these words, "A nation's school ... are an organ of its life, whose special function is to consolidate its spiritual strength, to maintain its historical continuity, to secure its past achievements, to guarantee its future. Through its schools a nation should become conscious of the abiding sources from which the best movements in its life have always taken their aspiration, should come to share the dreams of its nobler sons, should constantly submit itself to self-criticism, should purge its ideals, should reinform and redirect impulses".

9. *S. Balakrishna Joshi* sums up the concept of a school as, "A well-conducted school is a happy home, a sacred shrine, a social centre, and a society in miniature and a bewitching Brindavan, all beautifully blended into a synthetic structure."

10. *P.C. Wren* describes the functions of a school as "Organise the school to benefit the scholar, to train his faculties, to widen his outlook, cultivate his mind, to form and strengthen his character, to develop and cultivate his aesthetic sense, to build up his body, his health and strength, to teach him his duty to himself, to the community and the state, in short to make an honest, capable and healthy man of him—organise the school for this and not to prepare him for the matriculation examination".

11. *Harold Rugg* thinks of school as an "enterprise in living, both social and personal".

FUNCTIONS AND ROLES OF THE SCHOOL IN THE SOCIETY

The school is expected to perform the following functions and roles:

1. transmitter of cultural heritage of the society.
2. conserver of cultural heritage of the society.
3. promoter of cultural heritage of the society.
4. connecting link between home and the community.
5. provider of special environment for the all-round development of the child.
6. provider of a planned scheme of things for the child.
7. promoter of cultural pluralism, i.e., tolerance of all cultures.
8. promoter of ideals of the State.
9. promoter of social development of the child.
10. promoter of democratic values in the child.
11. promoter of secular values in the child.
12. promoter of ethical, moral and spiritual values of the child.

14. promoter of professional and vocational skills and values in the child.
15. promoter of egalitarian values in the child.
16. promoter of innate abilities of the child.
17. promoter of values of international understanding and peace.
18. centre of community.
19. trainer in the art of living together.

Summing up: In the words of S. Balakrishna Joshi, "In a word, a well-conducted school is a happy home, a sacred shrine, a social centre, a State in miniature and bewitching Brindavan—all beautifully blended into a synthetic structure".

MEASURES TO BE TAKEN BY THE SCHOOL TO PERFORM ITS FUNCTIONS

1. *Balanced and Simplified Environment*: The school discharges its several functions through curriculum. The school is envisaged to become an 'idealised miniature community'.

2. *Art of Living Together*: The school provides a number of group activities through which students get a lot of training in the art of living together.

3. *Training in Democratic Living*: School incorporates activities like student self-government.

4. *Opportunities for Vocational Training*: School includes several programmes and activities like work experience and vocational subjects.

5. *Development of Child's Entire Personality*: The school makes all possible efforts to provide a pleasant and stimulating intellectual, physical and spiritual environment which will evoke the manifold interests of the students and develop them creatively and constructively. It formulates a programme of hobbies, occupations and projects that cater to the varying aptitudes and temperaments of the students.

The school library, laboratory and workshop become the hub of stimulating activities.

6. *Spirit of Cooperation*: The head of school should develop an environment of cooperation and harmony among staff members so that the students also imbibe this attitude.

7. *Cooperation with Several Agencies of Education*: School enlists the cooperation of the various formal, non-formal and informal agencies wherever considered necessary.

8. *School as a Centre of Community Service*: School can organise adult education classes. It can take up community service programmes.

9. *Provision for School Experimentation*: The school laboratory will not be a toy-affair, where a few simple and carefully planned experiments are performed under vigilant eye of the teacher who sees that the prescribed routine is followed. It will endeavour to give them something of the thrill and joy of discovery and the educative experience of learning through trial and error.

10. *Opportunities for Self-Discipline*: Discipline in the school will not be a matter of arbitrary rules and regulations enforced through the authority of the teachers helped by the lure of reward or the fear of punishment. The students will be given full freedom to organise functions, to conduct many of the school activities through their own committees and even to deal with certain types of disciplinary cases. In this way, discipline will be maintained through the influence of the social group and it will gradually lead to the development of self-discipline.

11. *Development of Child's Entire Personality*: School should provide a richly varied pattern of activities to cater to the development of its children's entire personality. It has to formulate a scheme of hobbies, occupations and projects that will appeal to draw out hidden powers of children of varying temperaments and aptitudes.

12. *Provision of a Stimulating Environment*: The primary concern of the school should be to provide for its pupils a rich, pleasant and stimulating environment which will evoke their manifold interests and make life a matter of joyful experience.

13. *Transformation into Activity School*: The school must be transformed into an "activity school" because activity has an irresistible appeal for every normal child and is his natural path to the goal of knowledge and culture.

14. *Development of Scientific Outlook*: Emphasis on all school programmes should be laid in the development of scientific temper in the minds of the students. Needless to state that scientific temper is very conductive to social change.

FUNCTIONS OF THE SCHOOL IN BEHAVIOURAL TERMS:

Historical Letter of Abraham Lincoln To The Headmaster Of His Son's School

The word of wisdom stated more than one hundred years ago are still valid today. (extracts from letter)

> He will have to learn, I know that all men are not just, all men are not true. But teach him also that for every scoundrel, there is hero, that for every selfish politician, there is a dedicated leader.
>
> It will take time, I know; but teach him if you can, that a dollar earned is of more than five thousand.
>
> Teach him to learn to lose and also to enjoy winning.
>
> Steer him away from envy if you can.
>
> Teach him to learn that the bullies are the easiest to lick.
>
> Teach him if you can, the wonder of books but also give him quiet time to ponder over the eternal mystery of birds in the sky, bees in the sun and flowers on a green hillside.
>
> Teach him, it is far more honourable to fail than to cheat.
>
> Teach him to have faith in his own ideas, even if anybody tells him they are wrong.
>
> Teach him to be gentle with gentle people and tough with the tough.
>
> Try to give my son the strength not to follow the crowd when everyone is getting on the band-wagon.

Teach him to listen to all men. Teach him also to filter all he hears on a screen of truth and take on the good that comes through.

Teach him if you can, how to laugh when he is sad.

Teach him, there is no shame in tears.

Teach him to scoff at cynics and to beware of too much sweetness.

Teach him to sell his brawn and brain to the highest bidders, but never to put a price tag on his heart and soul.

Teach him to close his ears to a howling mob.

Teach him to stand and fight if he thinks he's right.

Teach him gently but do not cuddle him because only the tests of fire make fine steel.

Let him have the courage to be impatient. Let him have the patience to be brave.

Teach him always to have sublime faith in himself because then he will always have sublime faith in mankind.

Summing Up

In the words of *S. Bala Krishna Joshi*, "A school is not a mere brick and mortar structure housing a miscellany of pupils and teachers; a school is not a market place where knowledge is doled out to unwilling consumers of varying capacities; a school is not a railway platform where a heterogeneous crowd gathers with diverse objects; a school is not a vigorous reformatory where juvenile suspects are kept under vigilant watch; a school is a spiritual organism with a distinctive personality of its own, a school is a vibrant community centre, radiating life and energy all-round, a school is a wonderful edifice, resting on the foundation of goodwill—goodwill of the public, goodwill of the parents, goodwill of the pupils. In a word, a well-conducted school is a happy home, a sacred shrine, a social centre, a state in miniature and bewitching Brindavan, all beautifully blended into a synthetic structure."